KU-216-699

TO:

Righteous are you, O LORD…
Your promises have been thoroughly tested,
  and your servant loves them.

Psalm 119:137, 140

FROM:

ZONDERVAN

Promises for Graduates from the New International Version
Copyright © 2004 by Zondervan

Requests for information should be addressed to:

Zondervan, *Grand Rapids, Michigan 49530*

ISBN 978-0-310-80417-8

All Scripture quotations, unless otherwise indicated, are taken from the *Holy Bible, New International Version*®. NIV®. Copyright © 1973, 1978, 1984 by International Bible Society. Used by permission of Zondervan. All rights reserved.

All rights reserved. No part of this publication may be reproduced, stored in a retrieval system, or transmitted in any form or by any means — electronic, mechanical, photocopy, recording, or any other — except for brief quotations in printed reviews, without the prior permission of the publisher.

Compiler: Snapdragon Editorial Group, Inc
Associate Editor: Tom Dean
Project Manager: Val Buick
Design: Kimberly Visser

Printed in the United States of America

---

11 12 13 14 • 20 19 18 17 16 15 14 13 12 11 10 9 8

promises *for* GRADUATES

from the
New International Version

ZONDERVAN®

ZONDERVAN.com/
AUTHORTRACKER
follow your favorite authors

Dear Graduate:

The day you've been waiting for has finally arrived. You've completed the assignments, listened carefully to your teachers, and studied for and passed the exams. Now it's time to step out of the classroom and into the world.

As you go, be sure to take the Word of God with you. His precious promises are all intended to encourage, enlighten, and enrich your life and keep you on the path to a fulfilling future.

Take this little book with you, too. In it, we have brought together many wonderful promises on the topics you are sure to encounter in the years ahead. Read it and refer to it often. It will give you the edge you need as you begin your next adventure—pursuing your dreams.

Since we have these promises, dear friends, let us purify ourselves from everything that contaminates body and spirit, perfecting holiness out of reverence for God.

2 *Corinthians* 7:1

Table of Contents

Jesus said, "He who receives you receives me, and he who receives me receives the one who sent me. Anyone who receives a prophet because he is a prophet will receive a prophet's reward, and anyone who receives a righteous man because he is a righteous man will receive a righteous man's reward. And if anyone gives even a cup of cold water to one of these little ones because he is my disciple, I tell you the truth, he will certainly not lose his reward."

Matthew 10:40-42

Jesus said, "All that the Father gives me will come to me, and whoever comes to me I will never drive away."

John 6:37

I am always with you;
    you hold me by my right hand.
You guide me with your counsel,
    and afterward you will take me into glory.
Whom have I in heaven but you?

Psalm 73:23-25

This is what the LORD says...
"Fear not, for I have redeemed you;
    I have summoned you by name;
        you are mine."

Isaiah 43:1

Praise be to the God and Father of our Lord Jesus Christ, who...chose us in him before the creation of the world to be holy and blameless in his sight. In love he predestined us to be adopted as his sons through Jesus Christ, in accordance with his pleasure and will.

Ephesians 1:3-5

I have fought the good fight, I have finished the race, I have kept the faith. Now there is in store for me the crown of righteousness, which the Lord, the righteous Judge, will award to me on that day—and not only me, but also to all who have longed for his appearing.

2 *Timothy* 4:7-8

I press on to take hold of that for which Christ Jesus took hold of me. Brothers, I do not consider myself yet to have taken hold of it. But one thing I do: Forgetting what is behind and straining toward what is ahead, I press on toward the goal to win the prize for which God has called me heavenward in Christ Jesus. ... Only let us live up to what we have already attained.

Philippians 3:12-14, 16

Whatever was to my profit, I now consider loss for the sake of Christ. What is more, I consider everything a loss compared to the surpassing greatness of knowing Christ Jesus my Lord, for whose sake I have lost all things. I consider them rubbish, that I may gain Christ and be found in him, not having a righteousness of my own that comes from the law, but that which is through faith in Christ—the righteousness that comes from God and is by faith.

Philippians 3:7-9

LORD, you establish peace for us;
all that we have accomplished
you have done for us.

Isaiah 26:12

A longing fulfilled is a tree of life.

Proverbs 13:12

Wisdom is found in those who take advice.

Proverbs 13:10

"I will instruct you and teach you
in the way you should go;
I will counsel you and watch over you,"
says the LORD.

Psalm 32:8

Listen to advice and accept instruction,
and in the end you will be wise.

Proverbs 19:20

Jesus said, "The Counselor, the Holy Spirit, whom the Father will send in my name, will teach you all things and will remind you of everything I have said to you."

John 14:26

The way of a fool seems right to him,
but a wise man listens to advice.

Proverbs 12:15

This is what the LORD says:
"Stand at the crossroads and look;
ask for the ancient paths,
ask where the good way is, and walk in it,
and you will find rest for your souls."

Jeremiah 6:16

To God belong wisdom and power;
counsel and understanding are his.

Job 12:13

"Call to me and I will answer you and tell you great and unsearchable things you do not know," says the LORD.

Jeremiah 33:3

I will praise the LORD, who counsels me;
even at night my heart instructs me.
I have set the LORD always before me.
Because he is at my right hand,
I will not be shaken.

Psalm 16:7

Make it your ambition to lead a quiet life, to mind your own business and to work with your hands, just as we told you, so that your daily life may win the respect of outsiders and so that you will not be dependent on anybody.

1 Thessalonians 4:11-12

Make plans by seeking advice.

Proverbs 20:18

Where you have envy and selfish ambition, there you find disorder and every evil practice. But the wisdom that comes from heaven is first of all pure; then peace-loving, considerate, submissive, full of mercy and good fruit, impartial and sincere.

James 3:16-17

In his heart a man plans his course,
    but the LORD determines his steps.

Proverbs 16:9

Christ's love compels us, because we are convinced that one died forall, and therefore all died. And he died for all, that those who live should no longer live for themselves but for him who died for them and was raised again.

2 *Corinthians* 5:14-15

Aim for perfection, listen to my appeal, be of one mind, live in peace. And the God of love and peace will be with you.

2 *Corinthians* 13:11

Be all the more eager to make your calling and election sure. For if you do these things, you will never fall, and you will receive a rich welcome into the eternal kingdom of our Lord and Savior Jesus Christ.

2 *Peter* 1:10-11

The LORD has heard my weeping.
The LORD has heard my cry for mercy;
the LORD accepts my prayer.

Psalm 6:8-9

Jesus said, "I tell you the truth, my Father will give you whatever you ask in my name. Until now you have not asked for anything in my name. Ask and you will receive, and your joy will be complete."

John 16:23-24

"Before [my people] call I will answer;
while they are still speaking I will hear,"
says the LORD.

Isaiah 65:24

Jesus said, "Ask and it will be given to you; seek and you will find; knock and the door will be opened to you. For everyone who asks receives; he who seeks finds, and to him who knocks, the door will be opened."

Matthew 7:7-8

This is the confidence we have in approaching God: that if we ask anything according to his will, he hears us. And if we know that he hears us—whatever we ask—we know that we have what we asked of him."

1 John 5:14-15

In my distress I called to the LORD,
    and he answered me.
From the depths of the grave I called for help,
    and you listened to my cry.

Jonah 2:2

The LORD is near to all who call on him,
to all who call on him in truth.
He fulfills the desires of those who fear him;
he hears their cry and saves them.

Psalm 145:18-19

God will respond to the prayer of the destitute;
he will not despise their plea.
Let this be written for a future generation,
that a people not yet created may praise
the LORD.

Psalm 102:17-18

"Call to me and I will answer you and tell you great and unsearchable things you do not know," says the LORD.

Jeremiah 33:3

"Call upon me in the day of trouble;
I will deliver you, and you will honor me,"
declares the LORD.

Psalm 50:15

The LORD is far from the wicked
but he hears the prayer of the righteous.

Proverbs 15:29

Is anyone of you sick? He should call the elders of the church to pray over him and anoint him with oil in the name of the Lord. And the prayer offered in faith will make the sick person well; the Lord will raise him up. If he has sinned, he will be forgiven.

James 5:14-15

Your beauty should not come from outward adornment, such as braided hair and the wearing of gold jewelry and fine clothes. Instead, it should be that of your inner self, the unfading beauty of a gentle and quiet spirit, which is of great worth in God's sight.

1 Peter 3:3-4

Charm is deceptive, and beauty is fleeting;
but a woman who fears the LORD is to be
praised.
Give her the reward she has earned,
and let her works bring her praise
at the city gate.

Proverbs 31:30-31

The LORD does not look at the things man looks at. Man looks at the outward appearance, but the LORD looks at the heart.

1 Samuel 16:7

Dress modestly with decency and propriety; not with braided hair or gold or pearls or expensive clothes, but with good deeds, appropriate for women who profess to worship God.

1 Timothy 2:9-10

[The Messiah] had no beauty or majesty to
attract us to him,
nothing in his appearance that we should
desire him.
He was despised and rejected by men,
a man of sorrows, and familiar with suffering.
Like one from whom men hide their faces
he was despised, and we esteemed him not...
But he was pierced for our transgressions,
he was crushed for our iniquities;
the punishment that brought us peace
was upon him,
and by his wounds we are healed.

Isaiah 53:2-3, 5

God does not judge by external appearance.

Galatians 2:6

It is God who makes both us and you stand firm in Christ. He anointed us, set his seal of ownership on us, and put his Spirit in our hearts as a deposit, guaranteeing what is to come.

2 Corinthians 1:21-22

Jesus said, "My sheep listen to my voice; I know them, and they follow me. I give them eternal life, and they shall never perish; no one can snatch them out of my hand. My Father, who has given them to me, is greater than all; no one can snatch them out of my Father's hand."

John 10:27-29

Those who have served well gain an excellent standing and great assurance in their faith in Christ Jesus.

1 Timothy 3:13

"Though the mountains be shaken
and the hills be removed,
yet my unfailing love for you will not be shaken
nor my covenant of peace be removed,"
says the LORD, who has compassion on you.

Isaiah 54:10

Since we have confidence to enter the Most Holy Place by the blood of Jesus ... let us draw near to God with a sincere heart in full assurance of faith, having our hearts sprinkled to cleanse us from a guilty conscience and having our bodies washed with pure water.

Hebrews 10:19, 22

I am not ashamed, because I know whom I have believed, and am convinced that he is able to guard what I have entrusted to him for that day.

2 *Timothy* 1:12

Faith is being sure of what we hope for and certain of what we do not see.

Hebrews 11:1

I am convinced that neither death nor life, neither angels nor demons, neither the present nor the future, nor any powers, neither height nor depth, nor anything else in all creation, will be able to separate us from the love of God that is in Christ Jesus our Lord.

Romans 8:38-39

We want each of you to show this same diligence to the very end, in order to make your hope sure. We do not want you to become lazy, but to imitate those who through faith and patience inherit what has been promised.

Hebrews 6:11-12

Jesus declared, "All that the Father gives me will come to me, and whoever comes to me I will never drive away. For I have come down from heaven not to do my will but to do the will of him who sent me. And this is the will of him who sent me, that I shall lose none of all that he has given me, but raise them up at the last day.

John 6:37-39

God who began a good work in you will carry it on to completion until the day of Christ Jesus.

Philippians 1:6

The effect of righteousness will be quietness
and confidence forever.

Isaiah 32:17

Your attitude should be the same as that of Christ Jesus: Who, being in very nature God, did not consider equality with God something to be grasped, but made himself nothing, taking the very nature of a servant, being made in human likeness. And being found in appearance as a man, he humbled himself and became obedient to death—even death on a cross! Therefore God exalted him to the highest place and gave him the name that is above every name.

Philippians 2:5-9

What does the LORD require of you?
To act justly and to love mercy
and to walk humbly with your God.

Micah 6:8

You were taught, with regard to your former way of life, to put off your old self, which is being corrupted by its deceitful desires; to be made new in the attitude of your minds; and to put on the new self, created to be like God in true righteousness and holiness.

Ephesians 4:22-24

Above all else, guard your heart,
for it is the wellspring of life.

Proverbs 4:23

Whoever claims to live in God must walk as Jesus did.

1 John 2:6

Jesus said, "The greatest among you will be your servant. For whoever exalts himself will be humbled, and whoever humbles himself will be exalted."

Matthew 23:11-12

To all who received him, to those who believed in his name, he gave the right to become children of God—children born not of natural descent, nor of human decision or a husband's will, but born of God.

John 1:12-13

Believe in the Lord Jesus, and you will be saved—you and your household.

Acts 16:31

If you confess with your mouth, "Jesus is Lord," and believe in our heart that God raised him from the dead, you will be saved. For it is with your heart that you believe and are justified, and it is with your mouth that you confess and are saved.

Romans 10:9-10

Jesus said, "God so loved the world that he gave his one and only Son, that whoever believes in him shall not perish but have eternal life."

John 3:16

All the prophets testify about Jesus that everyone who believes in him receives forgiveness of sins through his name.

Acts 10:43

Jesus said, "Because you have seen me, you have believed; blessed are those who have not seen and yet have believed."

John 20:29

Without faith it is impossible to please God, because anyone who comes to him must believe that he exists and that he rewards those who earnestly seek him.

Hebrews 11:6

Though you have not seen Jesus Christ, you love him; and even though you do not see him now, you believe in him and are filled with an inexpressible and glorious joy, for you are receiving the goal of your faith, the salvation of your souls.

1 Peter 1:8-9

We ought always to thank God for you, brothers loved by the Lord, because from the beginning God chose you to be saved through the sanctifying work of the Spirit and through belief in the truth. He called you to this through our gospel, that you might share in the glory of our Lord Jesus Christ.

2 *Thessalonians* 2:13-14

Jesus said, "I tell you the truth, he who believes has everlasting life."

John 6:47

We also believe and therefore speak, because we know that the one who raised the Lord Jesus from the dead will also raise us with Jesus and present us with you in his presence.

2 Corinthians 4:13-14

Jesus said, "I am the resurrection and the life. He who believes in me will live, even though he dies; and whoever lives and believes in me will never die."

John 11:25-26

Whoever believes in him [Jesus Christ] is not condemned.

John 3:18

The man who looks intently into the perfect law that gives freedom, and continues to do this, not forgetting what he has heard, but doing it—he will be blessed in what he does.

James 1:25

The unfolding of your words gives light,
O God;
it gives understanding to the simple.

Psalm 119:130

Jesus said, "Blessed ... are those who hear the word of God and obey it."

Luke 11:28

Do your best to present yourself to God as one approved, a workman who does not need to be ashamed and who correctly handles the word of truth.

2 *Timothy* 2:15

I have hidden your word in my heart
that I might not sin against you, O Lord.

Psalm 119:11

We have the word of the prophets made more certain, and you will do well to pay attention to it, as to a light shining in a dark place, until the day dawns and the morning star rises in your hearts.

2 Peter 1:19

When your words came, I ate them;
  they were my joy and my heart's delight,
for I bear your name,
  O LORD God Almighty

Jeremiah 15:16

Jesus said, "It is written: 'Man does not live on bread alone, but on every word that comes from the mouth of God.'"

Matthew 4:4

Jesus said, "[Some people], like seed sown on good soil, hear the word, accept it, and produce a crop—thirty, sixty or even a hundred times what was sown."

Mark 4:20

Praise be to the God and Father of our Lord Jesus Christ, who has blessed us in the heavenly realms with every spiritual blessing in Christ.

Ephesians 1:3

Blessings crown the head of the righteous.

Proverbs 10:6

Surely, O LORD, you bless the righteous;
you surround them with your favor as
with a shield.

Psalm 5:12

There is no difference between Jew and Gentile—the same Lord is Lord of all and richly blesses all who call on him.

Romans 10:12

He who has clean hands and a pure heart,
who does not lift up his soul to an idol
or swear by what is false.
He will receive blessing from the LORD
and vindication from God his Savior.

Psalm 24:4-5

From the fullness of God's grace we have all received one blessing after another.

John 1:16

Blessed are those you choose
    and bring near to live in your courts!
We are filled with the good things of your house,
    of your holy temple.

Psalm 65:4

The LORD gives strength to his people;
    the LORD blesses his people with peace.

Psalm 29:11

"I will bless [my people] and the places surrounding my hill. I will send down showers in season; there will be showers of blessing. The trees of the field will yield their fruit and the ground will yield its crops; the people will be secure in their land. They will know that I am the LORD."

Ezekiel 34:26-27

I am setting before you today a blessing and a curse—the blessing if you obey the commands of the LORD your God that I am giving you today.

Deuteronomy 11:26-27

Looking at his disciples, Jesus said:
"Blessed are you who are poor,
for yours is the kingdom of God.
Blessed are you who hunger now,
for you will be satisfied.
Blessed are you who weep now
for you will laugh.
Blessed are you when men hate you,
when they exclude you and insult you
and reject your name as evil,
because of the Son of Man.
Rejoice in that day and leap for joy because great is your reward in heaven.

Luke 6:20-23

[The Lord said to his people Israel:] "I will make you into a great nation and I will bless you; I will make your name great and you will be a blessing. I will bless those who bless you, and whoever curses you I will curse; and all peoples on earth will be blessed through you."

Genesis 12:2-3

Blessed is he who comes in the name of
the LORD.
From the house of the LORD we bless you.

Psalm 118:26

Blessed is the nation whose God is the LORD,
the people he chose for his inheritance.

Psalm 33:12

Do not repay evil with evil or insult with insult, but with blessing, because to this you were called so that you may inherit a blessing.

1 *Peter* 3:9

"Maidens will dance and be glad,
young men and old as well.
I will turn their mourning into gladness;
I will give them comfort and joy instead
of sorrow," says the LORD.

Jeremiah 31:13

I delight greatly in the LORD;
my soul rejoices in my God.
For he has clothed me with garments of salvation
and arrayed me in a robe of righteousness,
as a bridegroom adorns his head like a priest,
and as a bride adorns herself with her jewels.

Isaiah 61:10

Praise his name with dancing
and make music to him with tambourine
and harp.
For the LORD takes delight in his people;
he crowns the humble with salvation.
Let the saints rejoice in this honor
and sing for joy on their beds.

Psalm 149:3-5

"Be glad and rejoice forever in what I will create,
for I will create Jerusalem to be a delight
and its people a joy.
I will rejoice over Jerusalem
and take delight in my people;
the sound of weeping and of crying
will be heard in it no more," says the LORD.

Isaiah 65:18-19

Praise God in his sanctuary;
praise him in his mighty heavens.
Praise him for his acts of power;
praise him for his surpassing greatness.
Praise him with the sounding of the trumpet,
praise him with the harp and lyre,
praise him with tambourine and dancing,
praise him with the strings and flute,
praise him with the clash of cymbals,
praise him with resounding cymbals.
Let everything that has breath
praise the LORD.

Psalm 150

Because the Sovereign LORD helps me,
    I will not be disgraced.
Therefore have I set my face like flint,
    and I know I will not be put to shame.

Isaiah 50:7

Strengthen your feeble arms and weak knees. "Make level paths for your feet," so that the lame may not be disabled, but rather healed.

Hebrews 12:12-13

For a little while you may have had to suffer grief in all kinds of trials. These have come so that your faith—of greater worth than gold, which perishes even though refined by fire—may be proved genuine and may result in praise, glory and honor when Jesus Christ is revealed.

1 Peter 1:6-7

Since we are surrounded by such a great cloud of witnesses, let us throw off everything that hinders and the sin that so easily entangles, and let us run with perseverance the race marked out for us. Let us fix our eyes on Jesus, the author and perfecter of our faith, who for the joy set before him endured the cross, scorning its shame, and sat down at the right hand of the throne of God. Consider him who endured such opposition from sinful men, so that you will not grow weary and lose heart.

Hebrews 12:1-3

Blessed is the man who perseveres under trial, because when he has stood the test, he will receive the crown of life that God has promised to those who love him.

James 1:12

Praise be to the name of God for ever and ever;
wisdom and power are his.
He changes times and seasons;
he sets up kings and deposes them.
He gives wisdom to the wise
and knowledge to the discerning.
He reveals deep and hidden things;
he knows what lies in darkness,
and light dwells with him.

Daniel 2:20-22

Jesus said, "I tell you the truth, unless you change and become like little children, you will never enter the kingdom of heaven."

Matthew 18:3

Be made new in the attitude of your minds.

Ephesians 4:23

Do not conform any longer to the pattern of this world, but be transformed by the renewing of your mind.

Romans 12:2

Though outwardly we are wasting away, yet inwardly we are being renewed day by day.

2 Corinthians 4:16

Our citizenship is in heaven. And we eagerly await a Savior from there, the Lord Jesus Christ, who, by the power that enables him to bring everything under his control, will transform our lowly bodies so that they will be like his glorious body.

Philippians 3:20-21

If anyone is in Christ, he is a new creation, the old has gone, the new has come!

2 Corinthians 5:17

You have taken off your old self with its practices and have put on the new self, which is being renewed in knowledge in the image of its Creator.

Colossians 3:9-10

The righteous will hold to their ways,
and those with clean hands will grow stronger.
Job 17:9

The LORD God is a sun and shield;
the LORD bestows favor and honor;
no good thing does he withhold
from those whose walk is blameless.
Psalm 84:11

A man's ways are in full view of the LORD,
and he examines all his paths.
Proverbs 5:21

The highway of the upright avoids evil;
he who guards his way guards his life.
Proverbs 16:17

We know that suffering produces perseverance; perseverance, character; and character, hope. And hope does not disappoint us, because God has poured out his love into our hearts by the Holy Spirit, whom he has given us.
Romans 5:3-5

A wife of noble character is her husband's crown.

Proverbs 12:4

Who is wise and understanding among you? Let him show it by his good life, by deeds done in the humility that comes from wisdom.

James 3:13

Our conscience testifies that we have conducted ourselves in the world, and especially in our relations with you, in the holiness and sincerity that are from God. We have done so not according to worldly wisdom but according to God's grace.

2 *Corinthians* 1:12

Set an example for the believers in speech, in life, in love, in faith and in purity.

1 *Timothy* 4:12

Remind the people to be subject to rulers and authorities, to be obedient, to be ready to do whatever is good.

Titus 3:1

God's household ... is the church of the living God, the pillar and foundation of the truth.

1 Timothy 3:15

It is God who gave some to be apostles, some to be prophets, some to be evangelists, and some to be pastors and teachers, to prepare God's people for works of service, so that the body of Christ may be built up until we all reach unity in the faith and in the knowledge of the Son of God and become mature, attaining to the whole measure of the fullness of Christ.

Ephesians 4:11-13

Christ is the head of the body, the church; he is the beginning and the firstborn from among the dead, so that in everything he might have the supremacy.

Colossians 1:18

Let the word of Christ dwell in you richly as you teach and admonish one another with all wisdom, and as you sing psalms, hymns and spiritual songs with gratitude in your hearts to God.

Colossians 3:16

You are the body of Christ, and each one of you is a part of it. And in the church God has appointed first of all apostles, second prophets, third teachers, then workers of miracles, also those having gifts of healing, those able to help others, those with gifts of administration, and those speaking in different kinds of tongues.

1 Corinthians 12:27-28

Obey your leaders and submit to their authority. They keep watch over you as men who must give an account.

Hebrews 13:17

The body is a unit, though it is made up of many parts; and though all its parts are many, they form one body. So it is with Christ. For we were all baptized by one Spirit into one body—whether Jews or Greeks, slave or free—and we were all given the one Spirit to drink.

1 Corinthians 12:12-13

Just as each of us has one body with many members, and these members do not all have the same function, so in Christ we who are many form one body, and each member belongs to all the others.

Romans 12:4-5

Let us not give up meeting together, as some are in the habit of doing, but let us encourage one another—and all the more as you see the Day approaching.

Hebrews 10:25

You are a chosen people, a royal priesthood, a holy nation, a people belonging to God, that you may declare the praises of him who called you out of darkness into his wonderful light.

1 *Peter* 2:9

My comfort in my suffering is this:
Your promise preserves my life, LORD.

Psalm 119:50

"As a mother comforts her child,
so will I comfort you," says the LORD.

Isaiah 66:13

Praise be to the God and Father of our Lord Jesus Christ, the Father of compassion and the God of all comfort, who comforts us in all our troubles, so that we can comfort those in any trouble with the comfort we ourselves have received from God.

2 Corinthians 1:3-4

The LORD is close to the brokenhearted
and saves those who are crushed in spirit.
Psalm 34:18

Even though I walk through the valley of the shadow of death,
I will fear no evil,
for you are with me, LORD;
your rod and your staff,
they comfort me.
Psalm 23:4

May your unfailing love be my comfort, O God,
according to your promise to your servant.
Psalm 119:76

"Blessed are those who mourn,
for they will be comforted."

Matthew 5:4

You turned my wailing into dancing;
you removed my sackcloth and
clothed me with joy,
that my heart may sing to you and not be silent.
O LORD my God, I will give you
thanks forever.

Psalm 30:11-12

The Lamb at the center of the throne will be their shepherd; he will lead them to springs of living water. And God will wipe away every tear from their eyes.

Revelation 7:17

I remember your ancient laws, O LORD,
and I find comfort in them.

Psalm 119:52

Give me a sign of your goodness,
that my enemies may see it and be put to shame,
for you, O LORD, have helped me and comforted me.

Psalm 86:17

Jesus said, "I am coming soon. Hold on to what you have, so that no one will take your crown. Him who overcomes I will make a pillar in the temple of my God. Never again will he leave it. I will write on him the name of my God and the name of the city of my God, the new Jerusalem, which is coming down out of heaven from my God; and I will also write on him my new name."

Revelation 3:11-12

Be joyful always; pray continually; give thanks in all circumstances, for this is God's will for you in Christ Jesus.

1 *Thessalonians* 5:16-18

Commit your way to the LORD;
trust in him and he will do this:
He will make your righteousness
shine like the dawn,
the justice of your cause like
the noonday sun.

Psalm 37:5-6

"I will give them singleness of heart and action, so that they will always fear me for their own good and the good of their children after them. I will make an everlasting covenant with them:
I will never stop doing good to them, and I will inspire them to fear me, so that they will never turn away from me," declares the LORD.

Jeremiah 32:39-40

Commit to the LORD whatever you do,
and your plans will succeed.

Proverbs 16:

Test everything. Hold on to the good. Avoid every kind of evil. May God himself, the God of peace, sanctify you through and through. May your whole spirit, soul and body be kept blameless at the coming of our Lord Jesus Christ. The one who calls you is faithful and he will do it.

1 *Thessalonians* 5:21-24

The eyes of the LORD range throughout the earth to strengthen those whose hearts are fully committed to him.

2 *Chronicles* 16:9

Watch out that you do not lose what you have worked for, but that you may be rewarded fully. Anyone who runs ahead and does not continue in the teaching of Christ does not have God; whoever continues in the teaching has both the Father and the Son.

2 John 8-9

Those who suffer according to God's will should commit themselves to their faithful Creator and continue to do good.

1 Peter 4:19

I know whom I have believed, and am convinced that he is able to guard what I have entrusted to him for that day.

2 Timothy 1:12

Confess your sins to each other and pray for each other so that you may be healed.

James 5:16

He who guards his lips guards his life.

Proverbs 13:3

From the fruit of his mouth a man's stomach
is filled;
with the harvest from his lips he is satisfied.

Proverbs 18:20

The mouth of the righteous man utters wisdom,
and his tongue speaks what is just.
The law of his God is in his heart;
his feet do not slip.

Psalm 37:30-31

He who holds his tongue is wise.
The tongue of the righteous is choice silver.

Proverbs 10:19-20

From the fruit of his lips a man enjoys
good things.

Proverbs 13:2

We will no longer be infants, tossed back and forth by the waves, and blown here and there by every wind of teaching and by the cunning and craftiness of men in their deceitful scheming. Instead, speaking the truth in love, we will in all things grow up into him who is the Head, that is, Christ.

Ephesians 4:14-15

May the words of my mouth and
the meditation of my heart
be pleasing in your sight, O LORD.

Psalm 19:14

Always be prepared to give an answer to everyone who asks you to give the reason for the hope that you have. But do this with gentleness and respect.

1 Peter 3:15

The tongue that brings healing is a tree of life.

Proverbs 15:4

Let your conversation be always full of grace, seasoned with salt, so that you may know how to answer everyone.

Colossians 4:6

The Sovereign LORD has given me an
instructed tongue,
to know the word that sustains the weary.

Isaiah 50:4

If anyone speaks, he should do it as one speaking the very words of God.

1 Peter 4:11

Set a guard over my mouth, O LORD;
keep watch over the door of my lips.

Psalm 141:3

If anyone is never at fault in what he says, he is a perfect man, able to keep his whole body in check.

James 3:2

A wise man's heart guides his mouth,
and his lips promote instruction.
Pleasant words are a honeycomb,
sweet to the soul and healing to the bones.

Proverbs 16:23-24

A gentle answer turns away wrath,
but a harsh word stirs up anger.
The tongue of the wise commends knowledge.

Proverbs 15:1-2

Be kind and compassionate to one another, forgiving each other, just as in Christ God forgave you. Be imitators of God, therefore, as dearly loved children and live a life of love, just as Christ loved us and gave himself up for us as a fragrant offering and sacrifice to God

Ephesians 4:32–5:2

Let your compassion come to me
that I may live,
for your law is my delight, O LORD.

Psalm 119: 77

The LORD longs to be gracious to you;
he rises to show you compassion.
For the LORD is a God of justice.
Blessed are all who wait for him!

Isaiah 30:18

You, O Lord, are a compassionate and
gracious God,
slow to anger and abounding in love and
faithfulness.

Psalm 86:15

The LORD is good to all;
he has compassion on all he has made.

Psalm 145:9

"Though the mountains be shaken
and the hills be removed,
yet my unfailing love for you will not be shaken
nor my covenant of peace be removed,"
says the LORD, who has compassion on you.

Isaiah 54:10

"I will betroth you to me forever;
I will betroth you in righteousness
and justice,
in love and compassion," says the LORD.

Hosea 2:19

Your compassion is great, O LORD;
preserve my life according to your laws.

Psalm 119:156

As a father has compassion on his children,
so the LORD has compassion on those who fear him.

Psalm 103:13

Because of the LORD's great love we are not consumed,
for his compassions never fail.
They are new every morning;
great is your faithfulness.

Lamentations 3:22-23

The LORD your God is gracious and compassionate. He will not turn his face from you if you return to him.

2 *Chronicles* 30:9

You will again have compassion on us, LORD;
you will tread our sins underfoot
and hurl all our iniquities into the depths
of the sea.

Micah 7:19

The LORD is gracious and compassionate.
He provides food for those who fear him;
he remembers his covenant forever.

Psalm 111:4-5

Even in darkness light dawns for the upright,
for the gracious and compassionate and
righteous man.

Psalm 112:4

Live in harmony with one another; be sympathetic, love as brothers, be compassionate and humble. Do not repay evil with evil or insult with insult, but with blessing, because to this you were called so that you may inherit a blessing.

1 Peter 3:8-9

The LORD will be your confidence
and will keep your foot from being snared.

Proverbs 3:26

The effect of righteousness will be quietness and confidence forever.

Isaiah 32:17

This is the confidence we have in approaching God: that if we ask anything according to his will, he hears us. And if we know that he hears us—whatever we ask—we know that we have what we asked of him.

1 John 5:14-15

Let us then approach the throne of grace with confidence, so that we may receive mercy and find grace to help us in our time of need.

Hebrews 4:16

Blessed is the man who trusts in the LORD,
whose confidence is in him.

Jeremiah 17:7

The LORD is the stronghold of my life—
of whom shall I be afraid? ...
Though an army besiege me,
my heart will not fear;
though war break out against me,
even then will I be confident.

Psalm 27:1, 3

Such confidence as this is ours through Christ before God. Not that we are competent in ourselves to claim anything for ourselves, but our competence comes from God.

2 Corinthians 3:4-5

Do not throw away your confidence; it will be richly rewarded.

Hebrews 10:35

God who began a good work in you will carry it on to completion until the day of Christ Jesus.

Philippians 1:6

I eagerly expect and hope that I will in no way be ashamed, but will have sufficient courage so that now as always Christ will be exalted in my body, whether by life or by death.

Philippians 1:20

The Lord said to me, "My grace is sufficient for you, for my power is made perfect in weakness." Therefore I will boast all the more gladly about my weaknesses, so that Christ's power may rest on me.

2 Corinthians 12:9

I can do everything through Christ who gives me strength.

Philippians 4:13

We have come to share in Christ if we hold firmly till the end the confidence we had at first.

Hebrews 3:14

If our hearts do not condemn us, we have confidence before God and receive from him anything we ask, because we obey his commands and do what pleases him. And this is his command; to believe in the name of his Son, Jesus Christ, and to love one another as he commanded us.

1 John 3:21-23

We say with confidence,
"The Lord is my helper; I will not be afraid.
What can man do to me?"

Hebrews 13:6

Pride only breeds quarrels,
but wisdom is found in those who
take advice.

Proverbs 13:10

It is to a man's honor to avoid strife.

Proverbs 20:3

Hatred stirs up dissension,
but love covers over all wrongs.

Proverbs 10:12

Jesus said, "I pray also for those who will believe in me through [my disciples'] message. .... May they be brought to complete unity to let the world know that you sent me."

John 17:20, 23

Agree with one another so that there may be no divisions among you.

1 Corinthians 1:10

A fool shows his annoyance at once,
but a prudent man overlooks an insult.

Proverbs 12:16

God has combined the members of the body ...so that there should be no division in the body, but that its parts should have equal concern for each other. If one part suffers, every part suffers with it; if one part is honored, every part rejoices with it.

1 Corinthians 12:24-26

Do everything without complaining and arguing, so that you may become blameless and pure, children of God without fault in a crooked and depraved generation, in which you shine like stars in the universe as you hold out the word of life.

Philippians 2:14-16

Do not be quickly provoked in your spirit.

Ecclesiastes 7:9

Make every effort to keep the unity of the Spirit.

Ephesians 4:3

Keep your lives free from the love of money and be content with what you have, because God has said,

"Never will I leave you;
never will I forsake you."

Hebrews 13:5

Better a little with righteousness
than much gain with injustice.

Proverbs 16:8

I have learned to be content whatever the circumstances. I know what it is to be in need, and I know what it is to have plenty. I have learned the secret of being content in any and every situation, whether well fed or hungry, whether living in plenty or in want. I can do everything through him who gives me strength.

Philippians 4:11-13

Godliness with contentment is great gain. ... If we have food and clothing, we will be content with that.

1 Timothy 6:6, 8

Better the little that the righteous have
 than the wealth of many wicked;
for the power of the wicked will be broken,
 but the LORD upholds the righteous.

Psalm 37:16-17

The fear of the LORD leads to life;
 Then one rests content, untouched by trouble.

Proverbs 19:23

Better one handful with tranquility
 than two handfuls with toil
 and chasing after the wind.

Ecclesiastes 4:6

Since we live by the Spirit, let us keep in step with the Spirit.

Galatians 5:25

God did not call us to be impure, but to live a holy life.

1 Thessalonians 4:7

This is what the LORD says:
"Stand at the crossroads and look;
ask for the ancient paths,
ask where the good way is, and walk in it,
and you will find rest for your souls."

Jeremiah 6:16

Walk in all the way that the LORD your God has commanded you, so that you may live and prosper and prolong your days in the land that you will possess.

Deuteronomy 5:33

We have not stopped praying for you and asking God to fill you with the knowledge of his will through all spiritual wisdom and understanding. And we pray this in order that you may live a life worthy of the Lord and may please him in every way: bearing fruit in every good work, growing in the knowledge of God.

Colossians 1:9-10

Be very careful then, how you live—not as unwise but as wise, making the most of every opportunity.

Ephesians 5:15-16

He who walks righteously
and speaks what is right,
who rejects gain from extortion
and keeps his hand from accepting bribes,
who stops his ears against plots of murder
and shuts his eyes against contemplating evil—
this is the man who will dwell on the heights,
whose refuge will be the mountain fortress.
His bread will be supplied,
and water will not fail him.

Isaiah 33:15-16

This is what the LORD Almighty says: "Give careful thought to your ways."

Haggai 1:5

Preserve sound judgment and discernment,
do not let them out of your sight;
they will be life for you,
an ornament to grace your neck.
Then you will go on your way in safety,
and your foot will not stumble;
when you lie down, you will not be afraid,
when you lie down, your sleep will
be sweet.

Proverbs 3:21-24

Commit your way to the LORD;
trust in him and he will do this:
He will make your righteousness shine like
the dawn,
the justice of your cause like the noonday sun.

Psalm 37:5-6

"Who has known the mind of the Lord that he may instruct him?" But we have the mind of Christ.

1 Corinthians 2:16

If any of you lacks wisdom, he should ask God, who gives generously to all without finding fault, and it will be given to him.

James 1:5

Trust in the LORD with all your heart
and lean not on your own understanding;
in all your ways acknowledge him,
and he will make your paths straight.

Proverbs 3:5-6

Jesus said, "I will ask the Father, and he will give you another Counselor to be with you forever—the Spirit of Truth."

John 14:16-17

Your enemy the devil prowls around like a roaring lion looking for someone to devour. Resist him, standing firm in the faith, because you know that your brothers throughout the world are undergoing the same kind of sufferings.

1 Peter 5:8-9

Let us not become weary in doing good, for at the proper time we will reap a harvest if we do not give up.

Galatians 6:9

Jesus said, "I am coming soon. Hold on to what you have, so that no one will take your crown."

Revelation 3:11

Because the Sovereign LORD helps me,
    I will not be disgraced.
Therefore have I set my face like flint,
    and I know I will not be put to shame.

Isaiah 50:7

Stand firm. Let nothing move you. Always give yourselves fully to the work of the Lord, because you know that your labor in the Lord is not in vain.

1 Corinthians 15:58

You need to persevere so that when you have done the will of God, you will receive what he has promised. For in just a very little while, "He who is coming will come and will not delay."

Hebrews 10:36-37

Watch your life and doctrine closely. Persevere in them, because if you do, you will save both yourself and your hearers.

1 Timothy 4:16

Be strong and do not give up, for your work will be rewarded.

2 Chronicles 15:7

To the Jews who had believed him, Jesus said, "If you hold to my teachings, you are really my disciples. Then you will know the truth, and the truth will set you free."

John 8:31-32

Jesus said to his disciples, "If anyone would come after me, he must deny himself and take up his cross and follow me. For whoever wants to save his life will lose it, but whoever loses his life for me will find it."

Matthew 16:24-25

Jesus said, "A new command I give you: Love one another. As I have loved you, so you must love one another. By this all men will know that you are my disciples, if you love one another."

John 13:34-35

Jesus said, "My sheep listen to my voice; I know them, and they follow me."

John 10:27

Correct me, LORD, but only with justice—not in your anger.

Jeremiah 10:24

Jesus said, "Whoever serves me must follow me; and where I am, my servant also will be. My Father will honor the one who serves me."

John 12:26

Jesus said, "I am the light of the world. Whoever follows me will never walk in darkness, but will have the light of life."

John 8:12

Jesus said, "This is to my Father's glory, that you bear much fruit, showing yourselves to be my disciples."

John 15:8

Do not make light of the Lord's discipline,
and do not lose heart when he rebukes you,
because the Lord disciplines those he loves,
and he punishes everyone he accepts as a son.
Endure hardship as discipline; God is treating
you as sons.

Hebrews 12:5-7

Blessed is the man you discipline, O LORD,
the man you teach from your law;
you grant him relief from days of trouble.

Psalm 94:12-13

He who heeds discipline shows the way to life,
but whoever ignores correction leads others
astray.

Proverbs 10:17

He who listens to a life-giving rebuke
will be at home among the wise.
He who ignores discipline despises himself,
but whoever heeds correction gains
understanding.

Proverbs 15:31-32

Our fathers disciplined us for a little while as they thought best; but God disciplines us for our good, that we may share in his holiness. No discipline seems pleasant at the time, but painful. Later on, however, it produces a harvest of righteousness and peace for those who have been trained by it.

Hebrews 12:10-11

Blessed is the man whom God corrects;
so do not despise the discipline of the
Almighty.
For he wounds, but he also binds up;
he injures, but his hands also heal.

Job 5:17-18

When we are judged by the Lord, we are being disciplined so that we will not be condemned with the world.

1 *Corinthians* 11:32

[Abraham] did not waver through unbelief regarding the promise of God, but was strengthened in his faith and gave glory to God, being fully persuaded that God had power to do what he had promised. This is why "it was credited to him as righteousness."

Romans 4:20-22

Jesus answered, "I tell you the truth, if anyone says to this mountain, 'Go, throw yourself into the sea,' and does not doubt in his heart but believes that what he says will happen, it will be done for him."

Mark 11:23

What if some did not have faith? Will their lack of faith nullify God's faithfulness? Not at all!

Romans 3:3-4

Be merciful to those who doubt.

Jude 22

Jesus said, "Do not set your heart on what you will eat or drink; do not worry about it. For the pagan world runs after all such things, and your Father knows that you need them. But seek his kingdom, and these things will be given to you as well."

Luke 12:29-31

See to it, brothers, that none of you has a sinful, unbelieving heart that turns away from the living God. But encourage one another daily, as long as it is called Today, so that none of you may be hardened by sin's deceitfulness. We have come to share in Christ if we hold firmly till the end the confidence we had at first.

Hebrews 3:12-14

Encourage one another and build each other up, just as in fact you are doing.

1 Thessalonians 5:11

You hear, O LORD, the desire of the afflicted;
you encourage them, and you listen
to their cry.

Psalm 10:17

May our Lord Jesus Christ himself and God our Father, who loved us and by his grace gave us eternal encouragement and good hope, encourage your hearts and strengthen you in every good deed and word.

2 *Thessalonians* 2:16-17

Everything that was written in the past was written to teach us, so that through endurance and the encouragement of the Scriptures we might have hope.

Romans 15:4

Jesus answered, "In this world you will have trouble. But take heart! I have overcome the world."

John 16:33

This I call to mind
    and therefore I have hope:
Because of the LORD's great love
        we are not consumed,
    for his compassions never fail.
They are new every morning;
    great is your faithfulness.

Lamentations 3:21-23

To you, O LORD, I lift up my soul;
    in you I trust, O my God.
Do not let me be put to shame,
    nor let my enemies triumph over me.
No one whose hope is in you
    will ever be put to shame.

Psalm 25:1-3

Jesus said, "This is eternal life: that they may know you, the only true God, and Jesus Christ, whom you have sent."

John 17:3

Jesus said, "The man who loves his life will lose it, while the man who hates his life in this world will keep it for eternal life."

John 12:25

This is the testimony: God has given us eternal life, and this life is in his Son. He who has the Son has life; he who does not have the Son of God does not have life.

1 *John* 5:11-12

Jesus said, "God so loved the world that he gave his one and only Son, that whoever believes in him shall not perish but have eternal life."

John 3:16

Now that you have been set free from sin and have become slaves to God, the benefit you reap leads to holiness, and the result is eternal life. For the wages of sin is death, but the gift of God is eternal life in Christ Jesus our Lord.

Romans 6:22-23

Jesus said to her, "I am the resurrection and the life. He who believes in me will live, even though he dies; and whoever lives and believes in me will never die."

John 11:25-26

Jesus said, "My sheep listen to my voice; I know them, and they follow me. I give them eternal life, and they shall never perish; no one can snatch them out of my hand."

John 10:27-28

Jesus said, "You are the light of the world. A city on a hill cannot be hidden. Neither do people light a lamp and put it under a bowl. Instead they put it on its stand, and it gives light to everyone in the house. In the same way, let your light shine before men, that they may see your good deeds and praise your Father in heaven."

Matthew 5:14-16

I pray that you may be active in sharing your faith, so that you will have a full understanding of every good thing we have in Christ.

Philemon 1:6

Jesus said, "Peace be with you! As the Father has sent me, I am sending you."

John 20:21

Jesus said, "All authority in heaven and on earth has been given to me. Therefore go and make disciples of all nations, baptizing them in the name of the Father and of the Son and of the Holy Spirit, and teaching them to obey everything I have commanded you. And surely I am with you always, to the very end of the age."

Matthew 28:18-20

I am not ashamed of the gospel, because it is the power of God for the salvation of everyone who believes.

Romans 1:16

Jesus said, "This gospel of the kingdom will be preached in the whole world as a testimony to all nations, and then the end will come."

Matthew 24:14

I wait for the LORD, my soul waits,
and in his word I put my hope.

Psalm 130:5

Wait for the LORD;
be strong and take heart
and wait for the LORD.

Psalm 27:14

I eagerly expect and hope that I will in no way be ashamed, but will have sufficient courage so that now as always Christ will be exalted in my body, whether by life or by death.

Philippians 1:20

You do not lack any spiritual gift as you eagerly wait for our Lord Jesus Christ to be revealed. He will keep you strong to the end, so that you will be blameless on the day of our Lord Jesus Christ.

1 Corinthians 1:7-8

Let us acknowledge the LORD;
    let us press on to acknowledge him.
As surely as the sun rises,
    he will appear;
he will come to us like the winter rains,
    like the spring rains that water the earth.

Hosea 6:3

In the morning, O LORD, you hear my voice;
    in the morning I lay my requests before you
    and wait in expectation.

Psalm 5:3

The people were waiting expectantly and were all wondering in their hearts if John might possibly be the Christ. John answered them all, "I baptize you with water. But one more powerful than I will come, the thongs of whose sandals I am not worthy to untie. He will baptize you with the Holy Spirit and with fire."

Luke 3:15-16

Faith is being sure of what we hope for and certain of what we do not see.

Hebrews 11:1

Build yourselves up in your most holy faith and pray in the Holy Spirit. Keep yourselves in God's love as you wait for the mercy of our Lord Jesus Christ to bring you to eternal life.

Jude 20-21

Through Christ you believe in God, who raised him from the dead and glorified him, and so your faith and hope are in God.

1 Peter 1:21

Jesus said, "I tell you the truth, anyone who has faith in me will do what I have been doing. He will do even greater things than these, because I am going to the Father."

John 14:12

Jesus said, "I tell you the truth, if you have faith as small as a mustard seed, you can say to this mountain, 'Move from here to there' and it will move. Nothing will be impossible for you."

Matthew 17:20

Since we have been justified through faith, we have peace with God through our Lord Jesus Christ, through whom we have gained access by faith into this grace in which we now stand. And we rejoice in the hope of the glory of God.

Romans 5:1-2

It is by grace you have been saved, through faith—and this not from yourselves, it is the gift of God—not by works, so that no one can boast.

Ephesians 2:8-9

These are the words of him who is the First and the Last, who died and came to life again, "I know your afflictions and your poverty—yet you are rich! ... Be faithful, even to the point of death, and I will give you the crown of life."

Revelation 2:8-10

To the faithful you show yourself faithful,
to the blameless you show yourself blameless.

2 *Samuel* 22:26

Let love and faithfulness never leave you;
bind them around your neck,
write them on the tablet of your heart.
Then you will win favor and a good name
in the sight of God and man.

Proverbs 3:3-4

God holds victory in store for the upright,
he is a shield to those whose walk is
blameless,
for he guards the course of the just
and protects the way of his faithful ones.

Proverbs 2:7-8

Love the LORD, all his saints!
The LORD preserves the faithful,
but the proud he pays back in full.

Psalm 31:23

The fruit of the Spirit is love, joy, peace, patience, kindness, goodness, faithfulness, gentleness and self-control. Against such things there is no law.

Galatians 5:22-23

The LORD loves the just
and will not forsake his faithful ones.

Psalm 37:28

Those who plan what is good find love and faithfulness.

Proverbs 14:22

The LORD is my light and my salvation—
whom shall I fear?
The LORD is the stronghold of my life—
of whom shall I be afraid?

Psalm 27:1-2

I sought the LORD, and he answered me;
he delivered me from all my fears.

Psalm 34:4

"Do not fear for I am with you;
do not be dismayed, for I am your God.
I will strengthen you and help you;
I will uphold you with my righteous
right hand."

Isaiah 41:10

You did not receive a spirit that makes you a slave again to fear, but you received the Spirit of sonship. And by him we cry, "*Abba*, Father." The Spirit himself testifies with our spirit that we are God's children.

Romans 8:15-16

There is no fear in love. But perfect love drives out fear.

1 John 4:18

The LORD has taken away your punishment;
he has turned back your enemy.
The LORD, the King of Israel, is with you;
never again will you fear any harm.

Zephaniah 3:15

Jesus said, "Do not be afraid, little flock, for your Father has been pleased to give you the kingdom."

Luke 12:32

Do not be afraid. Stand firm and you will see the deliverance the LORD will bring you today.

Exodus 14:13

Even though I walk
through the valley of the shadow of death,
I will fear no evil,
for you are with me, LORD;
your rod and your staff,
they comfort me.

Psalm 23:4

When I am afraid,
I will trust in you, O LORD.

Psalm 56:3

Let the word of Christ dwell in you richly as you teach and admonish one another with all wisdom, and as you sing psalms, hymns and spiritual songs with gratitude in your hearts to God.

Colossians 3:16

How good and pleasant it is
when brothers live together in unity!
It is like precious oil poured on the head,
running down on the beard,
running down on Aaron's beard,
down upon the collar of his robes.
It is as if the dew of Hermon
were falling on Mount Zion.
For there the LORD bestows his blessing,
even life forevermore.

Psalm 133

Jesus said, "Where two or three come together in my name, there am I with them."

Matthew 18:20

If we walk in the light, as God is in the light, we have fellowship with one another.

1 John 1:7

Live in harmony with one another; be sympathetic, love as brothers, be compassionate and humble. Do not repay evil with evil or insult with insult, but with blessing, because to this you were called so that you may inherit a blessing.

1 Peter 3:8-9

In humility consider others better than yourselves. Each of you should look not only to your own interests, but also to the interests of others.

Philippians 2:3-4

Let us ... make every effort to do what leads to peace and to mutual edification.

Romans 14:19

Let no debt remain outstanding, except the continuing debt to love one another, for he who loves his fellowman has fulfilled the law.

Romans 13:8

"Bring the whole tithe into the storehouse, that there may be food in my house. Test me in this," says the LORD Almighty, "and see if I will not throw open the floodgates of heaven and pour out so much blessing that you will not have room enough for it."

Malachi 3:10

Honor the LORD with your wealth,
with the firstfruits of all your crops;
then your barns will be filled to overflowing,
and your vats will brim over with new wine.

Proverbs 3:9-10

He who gathers money little by little makes it grow.

Proverbs 13:11

Keep your lives free from the love of money and be content with what you have, because God has said,

"Never will I leave you;
never will I forsake you."

Hebrews 13:5

A good man leaves an inheritance for his
children's children,
but a sinner's wealth is stored up for
the righteous.

Proverbs 13:22

Jesus said, "Watch out! Be on your guard against all kinds of greed; a man's life does not consist in the abundance of his possessions."

Luke 12:15

My God will meet all your needs according to his glorious riches in Christ Jesus.

Philippians 4:19

Blessed is he
 whose transgressions are forgiven,
 whose sins are covered.
Blessed is the man
 whose sin the LORD does not count
 against him
 and in whose spirit is no deceit.

Psalm 32:1-2

If we confess our sins, God is faithful and just and will forgive us our sins and purify us from all unrighteousness.

1 John 1:9

When you were dead in your sins and in the uncircumcision of your sinful nature, God made you alive with Christ. He forgave us all our sins, having canceled the written code, with its regulations, that was against us and that stood opposed to us; he took it away, nailing it to the cross.

Colossians 2:13-14

Jesus said, "If you forgive men when they sin against you, your heavenly Father will also forgive you."

Matthew 6:14

Jesus said, "When you stand praying, if you hold anything against anyone, forgive him, so that your Father in heaven may forgive you your sins."

Mark 11:25

Bear with each other and forgive whatever grievances you may have against one another. Forgive as the Lord forgave you.

Colossians 3:13

Peter came to Jesus and asked, "Lord, how many times shall I forgive my brother when he sins against me? Up to seven times?"
Jesus answered, "I tell you, not seven times, but seventy-seven times."

Matthew 18:21-22

It is for freedom that Christ has set us free. Stand firm, then, and do not let yourselves be burdened again by a yoke of slavery.

Galatians 5:1

The creation itself will be liberated from its bondage to decay and brought into the glorious freedom of the children of God.

Romans 8:21

The Lord is the Spirit, and where the Spirit of the Lord is, there is freedom.

2 *Corinthians* 3:17

Jesus said, "You will know the truth, and the truth will set you free."

John 8:32

The LORD sets prisoners free.

Psalm 146:7

Jesus said, "If the Son sets you free, you will be free indeed."

John 8:36

Now that you have been set free from sin and have become slaves to God, the benefit you reap leads to holiness, and the result is eternal life.

Romans 6:22

Live as free men, but do not use your freedom as a cover-up for evil; live as servants of God.

1 *Peter* 2:16

Through Christ Jesus the law of the Spirit of life set me free from the law of sin and death.

Romans 8:2

The man who looks intently into the perfect law that gives freedom, and continues to do this, not forgetting what he has heard, but doing it—he will be blessed in what he does.

James 1:25

Jesus said, "Greater love has no one than this, that he lay down his life for his friends. You are my friends if you do what I command. I no longer call you servants, because a servant does not know his master's business. Instead, I have called you friends, for everything that I learned from my Father I have made known to you."

John 15:13-15

A man of many companions may come to ruin,
but there is a friend who sticks closer than a brother.

Proverbs 18:24

Do not forsake your friend and the friend of your father.

Proverbs 27:10

As iron sharpens iron,
so one man sharpens another.

Proverbs 27:17

Two are better than one,
because they have a good return for
their work:
If one falls down,
his friend can help him up.
But pity the man who falls
and has no one to help him up!
Also, if two lie down together,
they will keep warm.
But how can one keep warm alone?
Though one may be overpowered,
two can defend themselves.
A cord of three strands is not quickly broken.

Ecclesiastes 4:9–12

Wounds from a friend can be trusted.

Proverbs 27:6

Be devoted to one another in brotherly love.
Honor one another above yourselves.

Romans 12:10

A friend loves at all times,
and a brother is born for adversity.

Proverbs 17:17

As it is written:
"No eye has seen,
no ear has heard,
no mind has conceived
what God has prepared for those who
love him"—
but God has revealed it to us by his Spirit.

The Spirit searches all things, even the deep things of God.

1 Corinthians 2:9-10

"I know the plans I have for you," declares the LORD, "plans to prosper you and not to harm you, plans to give you hope and a future."

Jeremiah 29:11

We are children of God, and what we will be has not yet been made known. But we know that when he appears, we shall be like him, for we shall see him as he is.

1 John 3:2

Listen, you who say, "Today or tomorrow we will go to this or that city, spend a year there, carry on business and make money." Why, you do not even know what will happen tomorrow. Instead, you ought to say, "If it is the Lord's will, we will live and do this or that."

James 4:13-15

I am convinced that neither the present nor the future, nor any powers, neither height nor depth, nor anything else in all creation, will be able to separate us from the love of God that is in Christ Jesus our Lord.

Romans 8:38-39

The meek shall inherit the land
and enjoy great peace.

Psalm 37:11

Jesus said, "Take my yoke upon you and learn from me, for I am gentle and humble in heart, and you will find rest for your souls."

Matthew 11:29

As God's chosen people, holy and dearly loved, clothe yourselves with compassion, kindness, humility, gentleness and patience.

Colossians 3:12

In your hearts set apart Christ as Lord. Always be prepared to give an answer to everyone who asks you to give the reason for the hope that you have. But do this with gentleness and respect.

1 Peter 3:15

A gentle answer turns away wrath.

Proverbs 15:1

The fruit of the Spirit is love, joy, peace, patience, kindness, goodness, faithfulness, gentleness and self-control. Against such things there is no law.

Galatians 5:22-23

Pursue righteousness, godliness, faith, love, endurance and gentleness. Fight the good fight of the faith.

1 *Timothy* 6:11-12

Your beauty should not come from outward adornment, such as braided hair and the wearing of gold jewelry and fine clothes. Instead, it should be that of your inner self, the unfading beauty of a gentle and quiet spirit, which is of great worth in God's sight.

1 *Peter* 3:3-4

Be completely humble and gentle; be patient, bearing with one another inlove.

Ephesians 4:2

Each man should give what he has decided in his heart to give, not reluctantly or under compulsion, for God loves a cheerful giver.

2 Corinthians 9:7

He who gives to the poor will lack nothing.

Proverbs 28:27

Jesus said, "When you give to the needy, do not let your left hand know what your right hand is doing, so that your giving may be in secret. Then your Father, who sees what is done in secret, will reward you."

Matthew 6:3-4

Jesus said, "Give, and it will be given to you. A good measure, pressed down, shaken together and running over, will be poured into your lap. For with the measure you use, it will be measured to you."

Luke 6:38

If there is a poor man among your brothers ... give generously to him and do so without a grudging heart; then because of this the LORD your God will bless you in all your work and in everything you put your hand to.

Deuteronomy 15:7, 10-11

Jesus said, "Which of you fathers, if your son asks for a fish, will give him a snake instead? Or if he asks for an egg, will give him a scorpion? If you then, though you are evil, know how to give good gifts to your children, how much more will your Father in heaven give the Holy Spirit to those who ask him!"

Luke 11:11-13

Jesus said, "Give to everyone who asks you, and if anyone takes what belongs to you, do not demand it back."

Luke 6:30

A generous man will prosper;
he who refreshes others will himself be refreshed.

Proverbs 11:25

The LORD is good and his love endures forever;
his faithfulness continues through
all generations.

Psalm 100:5

The word of the LORD is right and true;
he is faithful in all he does.

Psalm 33:4

Know therefore that the LORD your God is God; he is the faithful God, keeping his covenant of love to a thousand generations of those who love him and keep his commands.

Deuteronomy 7:9

All the ways of the LORD are loving and faithful
for those who keep the demands of his covenant.

Psalm 25:10

The Lord is faithful, and he will strengthen and protect you from the evil one.

2 *Thessalonians* 3:3

The LORD is faithful to all his promises
and loving toward all he has made.

Psalm 145:13

I will sing of the LORD's great love forever;
with my mouth I will make your faithfulness known through all generations.
I will declare that your love stands firm forever,
that you established your faithfulness in heaven itself.

Psalm 89:1-2

God, who has called you into fellowship with his Son Jesus Christ our Lord, is faithful.

1 Corinthians 1:9

If we confess our sins, God is faithful and just and will forgive us our sins and purify us from all unrighteousness.

1 John 1:9

Great is your love, higher than the heavens;
your faithfulness reaches to the skies.

Psalm 108:4

I am still confident of this:
I will see the goodness of the LORD
in the land of the living.

Psalm 27:13

How great is your goodness,
which you have stored up for those who fear you,
which you bestow in the sight of men.

Psalm 31:19

Taste and see that the LORD is good;
blessed is the man who takes refuge in him.

Psalm 34:8

The LORD is good,
a refuge in times of trouble.
He cares for those who trust in him.

Nahum 1:7

Good and upright is the LORD;
therefore he instructs sinners in his ways.
He guides the humble in what is right
and teaches them his way.

Psalm 25:8-9

The LORD is good to all;
he has compassion on all he has made.

Psalm 145:9

We know that in all things God works for the good of those who love him, who have been called according to his purpose.

Romans 8:28

The LORD is good to those whose hope
is in him,
to the one who seeks him.

Lamentations 3:25

The LORD is good and his love endures forever;
his faithfulness continues through
all generations.

Psalm 100:5

Give me a sign of your goodness,
that my enemies may see it and
be put to shame,
for you, O LORD, have helped me and
comforted me.

Psalm 86:17

Many are the woes of the wicked,
　but the LORD's unfailing love
　surrounds the man who trusts in him.

Psalm 32:10

How great is the love the Father has lavished on us, that we should be called children of God! And that is what we are!

1 John 3:1

God is love. Whoever lives in love lives in God, and God in him. In this way, love is made complete among us so that we will have confidence on the day of judgment, because in this world we are like him.

1 John 4:16-17

From everlasting to everlasting
　the LORD's love is with those
　　who fear him,
　and his righteousness with their children.

Psalm 103:17

God demonstrates his own love for us in this: While we were still sinners, Christ died for us.

Romans 5:8

Because of his great love for us, God, who is rich in mercy, made us alive with Christ even when we were dead in transgressions—it is by grace you have been saved.

Ephesians 2:4-5

This is how we know what love is: Jesus Christ laid down his life for us. And we ought to lay down our lives for our brothers.

1 John 3:16

Jesus replied, "He who loves me will be loved by my Father, and I too will love him and show myself to him."

John 14:21

Who is a God like you,
who pardons sin and forgives the transgression
of the remnant of his inheritance?
You do not stay angry forever
but delight to show mercy.

Micah 7:18

Because of his great love for us, God, who is rich in mercy, made us alive with Christ even when we were dead in transgressions.

Ephesians 2:4-5

Seek the LORD while he may be found;
call on him while he is near.
Let the wicked forsake his way
and the evil man his thoughts.
Let him turn to the LORD, and he will have mercy on him,
and to our God, for he will freely pardon.

Isaiah 55:6-7

God's mercy extends to those who fear him,
from generation to generation.

Luke 1:50

Praise be to the God and Father of our Lord Jesus Christ! In his great mercy he has given us new birth into a living hope through the resurrection of Jesus Christ from the dead.

1 Peter 1:3

God saved us, not because of righteous things we had done, but because of his mercy. He saved us through the washing of rebirth and renewal by the Holy Spirit.

Titus 3:5

I, by your great mercy,
will come into your house;
in reverence will I bow down
toward your holy temple, O LORD.

Psalm 5:7

Jesus said, "Be merciful just as your Father is merciful."

Luke 6:36

"I am merciful," declares the LORD,
"I will not be angry forever."

Jeremiah 3:12

I urge, you, brothers, in view of God's mercy, to offer your bodies as living sacrifices, holy and pleasing to God—this is your spiritual act of worship.

Romans 12:1

The LORD your God is a merciful God; he will not abandon or destroy you or forget the covenant with your forefathers, which he confirmed to them by oath.

Deuteronomy 4:31

You, O Lord, are a compassionate and
gracious God,
slow to anger, abounding in love and
faithfulness.
Turn to me and have mercy on me.

Psalm 86:15-16

The Lord is full of compassion and mercy.

James 5:11

Remember, O LORD, your great mercy and love,
for they are from of old.
Remember not the sins of my youth
and my rebellious ways;
according to your love remember me,
for you are good, O LORD.

Psalm 25:6-7

God says to Moses, "I will have mercy on whom I have mercy, and I will have compassion on whom I have compassion." It does not, therefore, depend on man's desire or effort, but on God's mercy.

Romans 9:15-16

The LORD said, "My Presence will go with you, and I will give you rest."

Exodus 33:14

Blessed are those who have learned to
acclaim you,
who walk in the light of your presence,
O LORD.

Psalm 89:15

Where can I go from your Spirit?
Where can I flee from your presence?
If I go up to the heavens, you are there;
if I make my bed in the depths, you
are there.
If I rise on the wings of the dawn,
if I settle on the far side of the sea,
even there your hand will guide me,
your right hand will hold me fast.

Psalm 139:7-10

You have made known to me the path of life,
O LORD;
you will fill me with joy in your presence,
with eternal pleasures at your right hand.

Psalm 16:11

Tremble, O earth, at the presence of the Lord,
at the presence of the God of Jacob,
who turned the rock into a pool,
the hard rock into springs of water.

Psalm 114:7-8

This, then is how we know that we belong to the truth, and how we set our hearts at rest in his presence whenever our hearts condemn us. For God is greater than our hearts, and he knows everything.

1 John 3:19-20

In my integrity you uphold me, LORD,
and set me in your presence forever.

Psalm 41:12

Do not conform any longer to the pattern of this world, but be transformed by the renewing of your mind. Then you will be able to test and approve what God's will is—his good, pleasing and perfect will.

Romans 12:2

In Christ we were also chosen, having been predestined according to the plan of God who works out everything in conformity with the purpose of his will, in order that we, who were the first to hope in Christ, might be for the praise of his glory.

Ephesians 1:11-12

The world and its desires pass away, but the man who does the will of God lives forever.

1 John 2:17

Jesus said, "My Father's will is that everyone who looks to the Son and believes in him shall have eternal life, and I will raise him up at the last day."

John 6:40

God made known to us the mystery of his will according to his good pleasure, which he purposed in Christ, to be put into effect when the times will have reached their fulfillment—to bring all things in heaven and on earth together under one head, even Christ.

Ephesians 1:9-10

Be joyful always; pray continually; give thanks in all circumstances, for this is God's will for you in Christ Jesus.

1 *Thessalonians* 5:16-18

The word of God is living and active. Sharper than any double-edged sword, it penetrates even to dividing soul and spirit, joints and marrow; it judges the thoughts and attitudes of the heart.

Hebrews 4:12

Jesus answered, "It is written: 'Man does not live on bread alone, but on every word that comes from the mouth of God.'"

Matthew 4:4

Your word is a lamp to my feet
and a light for my path, LORD.

Psalm 119:105

Jesus said, "Blessed rather are those who hear the word of God and obey it."

Luke 11:28

I have hidden your word in my heart, O LORD,
that I might not sin against you.

Psalm 119:11

Jesus said, "Heaven and earth will pass away, but my words will never pass away."

Mark 13:31

You have been born again, not of perishable seed, but of perishable, through the living and enduring word of God. For,

"All men are like grass,
and all their glory is like the flowers
of the field;
the grass withers and the flowers fall,
but the word of the Lord stands
forever."

1 *Peter* 1:23-25

The man who looks intently into the perfect law that gives freedom, and continues to do this, not forgetting what he has heard, but doing it—he will be blessed in what he does.

James 1:25

Who is going to harm you if you are eager to do good? But even if you should suffer for what is right, you are blessed.

1 Peter 3:13-14

Let us not become weary in doing good, for at the proper time we will reap a harvest if we do not give up. Therefore, as we have opportunity, let us do good to all people, especially to those who belong to the family of believers.

Galatians 6:9-10

Do not forget to do good and to share with others, for with such sacrifices God is pleased.

Hebrews 13:16

God "will give to each person according to what he has done." To those who by persistence in doing good seek glory, honor and immortality, he will give eternal life.

Romans 2:6-7

Trust in the LORD and do good;
dwell in the land and enjoy safe pasture.

Psalm 37:3

We are God's workmanship, created in Christ Jesus to do good works, which God prepared in advance for us to do.

Ephesians 2:10

Jesus said, "Let your light shine before men, that they may see your good deeds and glorify your Father in heaven."

Matthew 5:16

Anyone who does what is good is from God.

3 *John* 1:11

From the fullness of God's grace we have all received one blessing after another.

John 1:16

It is by grace you have been saved, through faith—and this not from yourselves, it is the gift of God—not by works, so that no one can boast. For we are God's workmanship, created in Christ Jesus to do good works, which God prepared in advance for us to do.

Ephesians 2:8-10

You know the grace of our Lord Jesus Christ, that though he was rich, yet for your sakes he became poor, so that you through his poverty might become rich.

2 *Corinthians* 8:9

Grace and peace be yours in abundance through the knowledge of God and of Jesus our Lord.

2 *Peter* 1:2

Let us then approach the throne of grace with confidence, so that we may receive mercy and find grace to help us in time of need.

Hebrews 4:16

God gives us more grace. That is why Scripture says: "God opposes the proud but gives grace to the humble."

James 4:6

The Lord said to me, "My grace is sufficient for you, for my power is made perfect in weakness." Therefore I will boast all the more gladly about my weaknesses, so that Christ's power may rest on me.

2 *Corinthians* 12:9

God is able to make all grace abound to you, so that in all things at all times, having all that you need, you will abound in every good work.

2 *Corinthians* 9:8

Jesus said, "Blessed are those who mourn,
for they will be comforted."

Matthew 5:4

Jesus said, "I tell you the truth, you will weep and mourn while the world rejoices. You will grieve, but your grief will turn to joy."

John 16:20

The LORD is close to the brokenhearted
and saves those who are crushed in spirit.

Psalm 34:18

The ransomed of the LORD will return.
They will enter Zion with singing;
everlasting joy will crown their heads.
Gladness and joy will overtake them,
and sorrow and sighing will flee away.

Isaiah 35:10

Remember your word to your servant, O LORD,
for you have given me hope.
My comfort in my suffering is this:
Your promise preserves my life.

Psalm 119:49-50

May your unfailing love be my comfort,
according to your promise to your servant,
LORD.
Let your compassion come to me that I may live
for your law is my delight.

Psalm 119:76-77

"I will refresh the weary and satisfy the faint," says the LORD.

Jeremiah 31:25

We do not want you to be ignorant about those who fall asleep, or to grieve like the rest of men, who have no hope. We believe that Jesus died and rose again and so we believe that God will bring with Jesus those who have fallen asleep in him.

1 Thessalonians 4:13-14

You turned my wailing into dancing;
you removed my sackcloth and clothed me
with joy, O God.

Psalm 30:11

Like newborn babies, crave pure spiritual milk, so that by it you may grow up in your salvation now that you have tasted that the Lord is good.

1 Peter 2:2–3

Grow in the grace and knowledge of our Lord and Savior Jesus Christ. To him be glory both now and forever!

2 *Peter* 3:18

Those who belong to Christ Jesus have crucified the sinful nature with its passions and desires. Since we live by the Spirit, let us keep in step with the Spirit.

Galatians 5:24–25

Do your best to present yourself to God as one approved, a workman who does not need to be ashamed and who correctly handles the word of truth.

2 *Timothy* 2:15

We will no longer be infants, tossed back and forth by the waves, and blown here and there by every wind of teaching and by the cunning and craftiness of men in their deceitful scheming. Instead, speaking the truth in love, we will in all things grow up into him who is the Head, that is, Christ.

Ephesians 4:14-15

Jesus said, "Whoever lives by the truth comes into the light, so that it may be seen plainly that what he has done has been done through God."

John 3:21

Jesus said, "I am the vine; you are the branches. If a man remains in me and I in him, he will bear much fruit; apart from me you can do nothing."

John 15:5

"I will instruct you and teach you in the way
you should go;
I will counsel you and watch over you,"
says the LORD.

Psalm 32:8

Teach me your way, O LORD,
and I will walk in your truth;
give me an undivided heart,
that I may fear your name.

Psalm 86:11

Good and upright is the LORD;
therefore he instructs sinners in his ways.
He guides the humble in what is right
and teaches them his way.

Psalm 25:8-9

The LORD will guide you always;
he will satisfy your needs in a sun-scorched land
and will strengthen your frame.
You will be like a well-watered garden,
like a spring whose waters never fail.

Isaiah 58:11

If I rise on the wings of the dawn,
    if I settle on the far side of the sea,
even there your hand will guide me,
    your right hand will hold me fast.

Psalm 139:9-10

Jesus said, "When he, the Spirit of truth, comes, he will guide you into all truth. He will not speak on his own; he will speak only what he hears, and he will tell you what is yet to come."

John 16:13

The LORD is my shepherd I shall not be in want.
    He makes me lie down in green pastures,
he leads me beside quiet waters,
    he restores my soul.
He guides me in paths of righteousness
    for his name's sake.

Psalm 23:1-3

O LORD my God, I called to you for help
and you healed me.
O LORD you brought me up from the grave,
you spared me from going down into the pit.

Psalm 30:2-3

Confess your sins to each other and pray for each other so that you may be healed.

James 5:16

A cheerful look brings joy to the heart,
and good news gives health to the bones.

Proverbs 15:30

Train yourself to be godly. For physical training is of some value, but godliness has value for all things, holding promise for both the present life and the life to come.

1 *Timothy* 4:7-8

Trust in the LORD with all your heart
    and lean not on your own understanding;
In all your ways acknowledge him,
    and he will make your paths straight.
Do not be wise in your own eyes;
    fear the LORD and shun evil.
This will bring health to your body
    and nourishment to your bones.

Proverbs 3:5-8

A heart of peace gives life to the body.

Proverbs 14:30

Do you not know that your body is a temple of the Holy Spirit, who is in you, whom you have received from God? You are not your own; you were bought at a price. Therefore honor God with your body.

1 Corinthians 6:19-20

The throne of God and of the Lamb will be in the city, and his servants will serve him. They will see his face, and his name will be on their foreheads. There will be no more night. They will not need the light of a lamp or the light of the sun, for the Lord God will give them light. And they will reign for ever and ever.

Revelation 22:3-5

Our citizenship is in heaven. And we eagerly await a Savior from there, the Lord Jesus Christ, who, by the power that enables him to bring everything under his control, will transfomour lowly bodies so that they will be like his glorious body.

Philippians 3:20-21

Jesus said, "In my Father's house are many rooms; if it were not so, I would have told you. I am going there to prepare a place for you. And if I go and prepare a place for you, I will come back and take you to be with me that you also may be where I am."

John 14:2-3

Now the dwelling of God is with men, and he will live with them. They will be his people, and God himself will be with them and be their God. He will wipe every tear from their eyes. There will be no more death or mourning or crying or pain, for the old order of things has passed away.

Revelation 21:3-4

Jesus said, "Rejoice that your names are written in heaven."

Luke 10:20

The Lord himself will come down from heaven, with a loud command, with the voice of the archangel and with the trumpet of God, and the dead in Christ will rise first. After that, we who are still alive and are left will be caught up together with them in the clouds to meet the Lord in the air. And so we will be with the Lord forever. Therefore encourage each other with these words.

1 Thessalonians 4:16–18

I looked and there before me was a great multitude that no one could count, from every nation, tribe, people and language, standing before the throne and in front of the Lamb. They were wearing white robes and were holding palm branches in their hands.

Revelation 7:9

If the earthly tent we live in is destroyed, we have a building from God, an eternal house in heaven, not built by human hands.

2 Corinthians 5:1

Never again will they hunger;
never again will they thirst.
The sun will not beat upon them,
nor any scorching heat.
For the Lamb at the center of the throne
will be their shepherd;
he will lead them to springs of living water.
And God will wipe away every tear from
their eyes.

Revelation 7:16–17

Nothing impure will ever enter [heaven], nor will anyone who does what is shameful or deceitful, but only those whose names are written in the Lamb's book of life.

Revelation 21:27

We say with confidence, "The Lord is my helper; I will not be afraid. What can man do to me?"

Hebrews 13:6

Because Christ himself suffered when he was tempted, he is able to help those who are being tempted.

Hebrews 2:18

It is the Sovereign LORD who helps me.
Who is he that will condemn me?
They will all wear out like a garment;
the moths will eat them up.

Isaiah 50:9

The LORD is my strength and my shield;
my heart trusts in him, and I am helped.
My heart leaps for joy
and I will give thanks to him in song.

Psalm 28:7

God is our refuge and strength,
an ever-present help in trouble.

Psalm 46:1

Surely the arm of the LORD is not too
short to save,
nor his ear too dull to hear.

Isaiah 59:1

God will deliver the needy who cry out,
the afflicted who have no one to help.

Psalm 72:12

The victim commits himself to you;
you are the helper of the fatherless.

Psalm 10:14

We wait in hope for the LORD;
he is our help and our shield.

Psalm 33:20

The Spirit helps us in our weakness. We do not know what we ought to pray for, but the Spirit himself intercedes for us with groans that words cannot express.

Romans 8:26

Make every effort to live in peace with all men and to be holy; without holiness no one will see the Lord.

Hebrews 12:14

Since we have these promises, dear friends, let us purify ourselves from everything that contaminates body and spirit, perfecting holiness out of reverence for God.

2 *Corinthians* 7:1

There is no one holy like the LORD;
there is no one besides you;
there is no Rock like our God.

1 *Samuel* 2:2

Do not conform to the evil desires you had when you lived in ignorance. But just as God who called you is holy, so be holy in all you do; for it is written: "Be holy, because I am holy."

1 *Peter* 1:14-16

God chose us in [Christ] before the creation of the world to be holy and blameless in his sight.

Ephesians 1:4

You ought to live holy and godly lives as you look forward to the day of God and speed its coming.

2 Peter 3:11-12

Once you were alienated from God and were enemies in your minds because of your evil behavior. But now he has reconciled you by Christ's physical body through death to present you holy in his sight, without blemish and free from accusation—if you continue in your faith, established and firm, not moved from the hope held out in the gospel.

Colossians 1:21-23

Do not believe every spirit, but test the spirits to see whether they are from God. ... This is how you can recognize the Spirit of God: Every spirit that acknowledges that Jesus Christ has come in the flesh is from God.

1 John 4:1-2

Jesus said, "I will ask the Father and he will give you another Counselor to be with you forever—the Spirit of truth. The world cannot accept him, because it neither sees him nor knows him. But you know him for he lives with you and will be in you."

John 14:16-17

The Lord is the Spirit and where the Spirit of the Lord is, there is freedom.

2 *Corinthians* 3: 17

Repent and be baptized, every one of you, in the name of Jesus Christ for the forgiveness of your sins. And you will receive the gift of the Holy Spirit. The promise is for you and your children and for all who are far off—for all whom the Lord our God will call.

Acts 2:38-39

You also were included in Christ when you heard the word of truth, the gospel of your salvation. Having believed, you were marked in him with a seal, the promised Holy Spirit, who is a deposit guaranteeing our inheritance until the redemption of those who are God's possession.

Ephesians 1:13-14

An honest answer
is like a kiss on the lips.

Proverbs 24:26

Whoever of you loves life
and desires to see many good days,
keep your tongue from evil
and your lips from speaking lies.

Psalm 34:12-13

A truthful witness gives honest testimony.

Proverbs 12:17

Truthful lips endure forever.

Proverbs 12:19

The LORD detests lying lips,
but he delights in men who are truthful.

Proverbs 12:22

Whatever is true, whatever is noble, whatever is right, whatever is pure, whatever is lovely, whatever is admirable—if anything is excellent or praiseworthy—think about such things.

Philippians 4:8

He who walks righteously
and speaks what is right,
who rejects gain from extortion
and keeps his hand from accepting bribes,
who stops his ears against plots of murder
and shuts his eyes against contemplating
evil—
this is the man who will dwell on the heights,
whose refuge will be the mountain fortress.
His bread will be supplied,
and water will not fail him.

Isaiah 33:15-16

No one whose hope is in you
will ever be put to shame.

Psalm 25:3

May the God of hope fill you with all joy and peace as you trust in him, so that you may overflow with hope by the power of the Holy Spirit.

Romans 15:13

Those who hope in the LORD
will renew their strength.
They will soar on wings like eagles;
they will run and not grow weary,
they will walk and not be faint.

Isaiah 40:31

We have put our hope in the living God, who is the Savior of all men, and especially of those who believe.

1 Timothy 4:10

We rejoice in the hope of the glory of God. Not only so, but we also rejoice in our sufferings, because we know that suffering produces perseverance; perseverance, character; and character, hope. And hope does not disappoint us, because God has poured out his love into our hearts by the Holy Spirit, whom he has given us.

Romans 5:2-5

Know also that wisdom is sweet to your soul;
if you find it, there is a future hope for you,
and your hope will not be cut off.

Proverbs 24:14

Set your hope fully on the grace to be given you when Jesus Christ is revealed.

1 Peter 1:13

Jesus said, "The greatest among you will be your servant. For whoever exalts himself will be humbled, and whoever humbles himself will be exalted."

Matthew 23:11-12

Do not think of yourself more highly than you ought, but rather think of yourself with sober judgment, in accordance with the measure of faith God has given you.

Romans 12:3

Humility and the fear of the LORD
bring wealth and honor and life.

Proverbs 22:4

Humble yourselves before the Lord, and he will lift you up.

James 4:10

All of you, clothe yourselves with humility toward one another, because, "God opposes the proud but gives grace to the humble." Humble yourselves, therefore, under God's mighty hand, that he may lift you up in due time.

1 Peter 5:5-6

The LORD takes delight in his people;
he crowns the humble with salvation.

Psalm 149:4

The LORD sustains the humble
but casts the wicked to the ground.

Psalm 147:6

A man's pride brings him low,
but a man of lowly spirit gains honor.

Proverbs 29:23

God guides the humble in what is right
and teaches them his way.

Psalm 25:9

Know that the LORD is God.
It is he who made us, and we are his;
we are his people, the sheep of his pasture.

Psalm 100:3

We are God's workmanship, created in Christ Jesus to do good works, which God prepared in advance for us to do.

Ephesians 2:10

You are a chosen people, a royal priesthood, a holy nation, a people belonging to God, that you may declare the praises of him who called you out of darkness into his wonderful light.

1 Peter 2:9

Now, this is what the LORD says—
"Fear not, for I have redeemed you;
I have summoned you by name; you are mine."

Isaiah 43:1

You also were included in Christ when you heard the word of truth, the gospel of your salvation. Having believed, you were marked in him with a seal, the promised Holy Spirit, who is a deposit guaranteeing our inheritance until the redemption of those who are God's possession.

Ephesians 1:13-14

For the sake of his great name the LORD will not reject his people, because the LORD was pleased to make you his own.

1 *Samuel* 12:22

Come, let us bow down in worship,
    let us kneel before the LORD our Maker;
for he is our God
    and we are the people of his pasture,
    the flock under his care.

Psalm 95:6-7

I know, my God, that you test the heart and are pleased with integrity.

1 Chronicles 29:17

Those who walk uprightly
enter into peace.

Isaiah 57:2

When a man's ways are pleasing to the LORD,
he makes even his enemies live at peace
with him.

Proverbs 16:7

The LORD God is a sun and shield;
the LORD bestows favor and honor;
no good thing does he withhold
from those whose walk is blameless.

Psalm 84:11

Jesus said, "Whoever can be trusted with very little can also be trusted with much, and whoever is dishonest with very little will also be dishonest with much."

Luke 16:10

God holds victory in store for the upright,
he is a shield to those whose walk is blameless,
For he guards the course of the just
and protects the way of his faithful ones.

Proverbs 2:7-8

Righteousness guards the man of integrity.

Proverbs 13:6

In my integrity you uphold me
and set me in your presence forever.

Psalm 41:12

The righteous man leads a blameless life;
blessed are his children after him.

Proverbs 20:7

Vindicate me, O LORD,
for I have led a blameless life;
I have trusted in the LORD
without wavering.
Test me, O LORD, and try me,
examine my heart and my mind;
for your love is ever before me.

Psalm 26:1-3

The angel said to her, "Mary, you have found favor with God. You will be with child and give birth to a son, and you are to give him the name Jesus. He will be great and will be called the Son of the Most High. ...

"How will this be," Mary asked the angel, "since I am a virgin?"

The angel answered, "The Holy Spirit will come upon you, and the power of the Most High will overshadow you. So the holy one to be born will be called the Son of God."

Luke 1:30-32, 34-35

In Christ all the fullness of the Deity lives in bodily form, and you have been given fullness in Christ, who is the head over every power and authority.

Colossians 2:9-10

Our citizenship is in heaven. And we eagerly await a Savior from there, the Lord Jesus Christ, who, by the power that enable him to bring everything under his control, will transform our lowly bodies so that they will be like his glorious body.

Philippians 3:20-21

Jesus Christ is the same yesterday, today and forever.

Hebrews 13:8

Christ is the mediator of a new covenant, that those who are called may receive the promised eternal inheritance—now that he has died as a ransom to set them free from the sins committed under the first covenant.

Hebrews 9:15

This is how we know what love is: Jesus Christ laid down his life for us.

1 John 3:16

Your statutes are my heritage forever, O LORD,
they are the joy of my heart.

Psalm 119:111

Those who sow in tears
will reap with songs of joy.

Psalm 126:5

You will go out in joy
and be led forth in peace;
the mountains and hills
will burst into song before you,
and all the trees of the field
will clap their hands.

Isaiah 55:12

Jesus said, "Until now you have not asked for anything in my name. Ask and you will receive, and your joy will be complete."

John 16:24

God will yet fill your mouth with laughter
and your lips with shouts of joy.

Job 8:21

The joy of the LORD is your strength.

Nehemiah 8:10

You have made known to me the path of life,
LORD;
you will fill me with joy in your presence,
with eternal pleasures at your right hand.

Psalm 16:11

Though you have not seen Jesus, you love him; and even though you do not see him now, you believe in him and are filled with an inexpressible and glorious joy, for you are receiving the goal of your faith, the salvation of your souls.

1 Peter 1:8-9

Let all who take refuge in you be glad,
O LORD;
Let them ever sing for joy.

Psalm 5:11

The precepts of the LORD are right,
giving joy to the heart.

Psalm 19:8

Consider it pure joy, my brothers, whenever you face trails of many kinds, because you know that the testing of your faith develops perseverance.

James 1:2-3

The LORD your God will bless you in all your harvest and in all the work of your hands, and your joy will be complete.

Deuteronomy 16:15

You turned my wailing into dancing;
you removed my sackcloth and clothed me
with joy,
that my heart may sing to you and not be silent.
O LORD my God, I will give thanks forever.

Psalm 30:11-12

You make me glad by your deeds, O LORD;
I sing for joy at the works of our hands.

Psalm 92:4

Tremble before him, all the earth!
The world is firmly established; it cannot be moved.
Let the heavens rejoice, let the earth be glad;
let them say among the nations,
"The LORD reigns!"
Let the sea resound, and all that is in it;
let the fields be jubilant, and everything in them!
Then the trees of the forest will sing,
they will sing for joy before the LORD,
for he comes to judge the earth.

1 Chronicles 16:30-33

Light is shed upon the righteous
and joy on the upright in heart.

Psalm 97:11

The LORD is a God of justice.
Blessed are all who wait for him!

Isaiah 30:18

Commit your way to the LORD;
trust in him and he will do this:
He will make your righteousness shine like the dawn,
the justice of your cause like the noonday sun.

Psalm 37:5-6

Many seek an audience with a ruler,
but it is from the LORD that man gets justice.

Proverbs 29:26

God's judgment is right, and as a result you will be counted worthy of the kingdom of God.

2 *Thessalonians* 1:5

The LORD is righteous,
he loves justice;
upright men will see his face.

Psalm 11:7

Speak up for those who cannot speak for
themselves,
for the rights of all who are destitute.
Speak up and judge fairly;
defend the rights of the poor and needy.

Proverbs 31:8-9

Learn to do right!
Seek justice,
encourage the oppressed.
Defend the case of the fatherless,
plead the case of the widow.

Isaiah 1:17

The LORD loves the just
and will not forsake his faithful ones.
They will be protected forever.

Psalm 37:28

God has showed you, O man, what is good.
And what does the LORD require of you?
To act justly and to love mercy
and to walk humbly with your God.

Micah 6:8

He who is kind to the poor lends to the LORD,
and he will reward him for what he has done.

Proverbs 19:17

Be kind and compassionate to one another, forgiving each other, just as in Christ God forgave you. Be imitators of God, therefore, as dearly loved children and live a life of love, just as Christ loved us and gave himself up for us as a fragrant offering and sacrifice to God

Ephesians 4:32–5:2

Make every effort to add to your faith goodness; and to goodness, knowledge; and to knowledge, self-control; and to self-control, perseverance; and to perseverance, godliness; and to godliness, brotherly kindness; and to brotherly kindness, love.

2 *Peter* 1:5–7

Make sure that nobody pays back wrong for wrong, but always try to be kind to each other and to everyone else.

1 Thessalonians 5:15

Carry each other's burdens, and in this way you will fulfill the law of Christ.

Galatians 6:2

Love is patient, love is kind.

1 Corinthians 13:4

As God's chosen people, holy and dearly loved, clothe yourselves with compassion, kindness, humility, gentleness and patience.

Colossians 3:12

When the kindness and love of God our Savior appeared, he saved us, not because of righteous things we had done, but because of his mercy.

Titus 3:4–5

God has rescued us from the dominion of darkness and brought us into the kingdom of the Son he loves, in whom we have redemption, the forgiveness of sin.

Colossians 1:13-14

The kingdom of God is not a matter of eating and drinking, but of righteousness, peace and joy in the Holy Spirit, because anyone who serves Christ in this way is pleasing to God and approved by men.

Romans 14:17-18

Since we are receiving a kingdom that cannot be shaken, let us be thankful, and so worship God acceptably with reverence and awe.

Hebrews 12:28

Jesus said, "Do not be afraid, little flock, for your Father has been pleased to give you the kingdom."

Luke 12:32

"I tell you the truth," Jesus said to [the disciples], "No one who has left home or wife or brothers or parents or children for the sake of the kingdom of God will fail to receive many times as much in this age and, in the age to come, eternal life."

Luke 18:29-30

Make every effort to add to your faith goodness; and to goodness, knowledge; and to knowledge, self-control; and to self-control, perseverance; and to perseverance, godliness; and to godliness, brotherly kindness; and to brotherly kindness, love. ... If you do these things, you will never fall, and you will receive a rich welcome into the eternal kingdom of our Lord and Savior Jesus Christ.

2 *Peter* 1:5-7, 10-11

This is my prayer: that your love may abound more and more in knowledge and depth of insight, so that you may be able to discern what is best and may be pure and blameless until the day of Christ.

Philippians 1:9-10

Grace and peace be yours in abundance through the knowledge of God and of Jesus Christ. His divine power has given us everything we need for life and godliness through our knowledge of him who called us by his own glory and goodness.

2 *Peter* 1:2-3

Grow in the grace and knowledge of our Lord and Savior Jesus Christ.

2 *Peter* 3:18

The prudent are crowned with knowledge.

Proverbs 14:18

To the man who pleases him, God gives wisdom, knowledge and happiness, but to the sinner he gives the task of gathering and storing up wealth to hand it over to the one who pleases God.

Ecclesiastes 2:26

Since the day we heard about you, we have not stopped praying for you and asking God to fill you with the knowledge of his will through all spiritual wisdom and understanding.

Colossians 1:9

Thanks be to God, who always leads us in triumphal procession in Christ and through us spreads everywhere the fragrance of the knowledge of him.

2 *Corinthians* 2:14

Knowledge of the Holy One is understanding.

Proverbs 9:10

Jesus said, "I am the resurrection and the life. He who believes in me will live, even though he dies; and whoever lives and believes in me will never die."

John 11:25-26

Jesus said, "The Spirit gives life; the flesh counts for nothing. The words I have spoken to you are spirit and they are life."

John 6:63

Set your hearts on things above, where Christ is seated at the right hand of God. Set your minds on things above, not on earthly things. For you died, and your life is now hidden with Christ in God. When Christ, who is your life, appears, then you also will appear with him in glory.

Colossians 3:1-4

You have made known to me the paths of life;
Lord;
you will fill me with joy in your presence.

Acts 2:28

With you is the fountain of life, O God;
in your light we see light.

Psalm 36:9

Jesus declared, "I am the bread of life. He who comes to me will never go hungry, and he who believes in me will never be thirsty."

John 6:35

If the Spirit of him who raised Jesus from the dead is living in you, he who raised Christ from the dead will also give life to your mortal bodies through his Spirit, who lives in you.

Romans 8:11

The fear of the LORD adds length to life.

Proverbs 10:27

God has said,
"Never will I leave you;
never will I forsake you."

Hebrews 13:5

In Christ we who are many form one body, and each member belongs to all the others.

Romans 12:5

The LORD your God goes with you; he will never leave you nor forsake you.

Deuteronomy 31:6

Jesus said, "I will not leave you as orphans; I will come to you."

John 14:18

Now the dwelling of God is with men, and he will live with them. They will be his people, and God himself will be with them and be their God. He will wipe every tear from their eyes.

Revelation 21:3-4

Sing to God, sing praise to his name,
    extol him who rides on the clouds—
his name is the LORD—
    and rejoice before him.
A father to the fatherless, a defender of widows,
    is God in his holy dwelling.
God sets the lonely in families,
    he leads forth the prisoners with singing.

Psalm 68:4-6

I am convinced that neither the present nor the future, nor any powers, neither height nor depth, nor anything else in all creation, will be able to separate us from the love of God that is in Christ Jesus our Lord.

Romans 8:38-39

I am always with you, LORD,
    you hold me by my right hand.

Psalm 73:23

Jesus replied, "If anyone loves me, he will obey my teaching. My Father will love him, and we will come to him and make our home with him."

John 14:23

"Because he loves me," says the LORD,
"I will rescue him;
I will protect him, for he acknowledges
my name."

Psalm 91:14

Jesus said, "'Love the Lord your God with all your heart and with all your soul and with all your mind and with all your strength.' The second [commandment] is this: 'Love your neighbor as yourself.' There is no commandment greater than these."

Mark 12:30-31

This is love for God: to obey his commands. And his commands are not burdensome.

1 *John* 5:3

Love the LORD your God, listen to his voice, and hold fast to him. For the LORD is your life.

Deuteronomy 30:20

Jesus said, "Whoever has my commands and obeys them, he is the one who loves me. He who loves me will be loved by my Father, and I too will love him and show myself to him."

John 14:21

We know that in all things God works for the good of those who love him, who have been called according to his purpose.

Romans 8:28

Anyone who does not love his brother, whom he has seen, cannot love God, whom he has not seen. And God has given us this command: Whoever loves God must also love his brother.

1 *John* 4:20-21

As God's chosen people, holy and dearly loved, clothe yourselves with compassion, kindness, humility, gentleness and patience. Bear with each other and forgive whatever grievances you may have against one another. Forgive as the Lord forgave you. And over all these virtues put on love, which binds them all together in perfect unity.

Colossians 3:12-14

About brotherly love we do not need to write to you, for you yourselves have been taught by God to love each other.

1 Thessalonians 4:9

Dear friends, let us love one another for love comes from God. Everyone who loves has been born of God and knows God.

1 John 4:7

Be devoted to one another in brotherly love. Honor one another above yourselves.

Romans 12:10

May the Lord make your love increase and overflow for each other and for everyone else.

1 *Thessalonians* 3:12

Live in harmony with one another; be sympathetic, love as brothers, be compassionate and humble.

1 *Peter* 3:8

No one has ever seen God; but if we love one another, God lives in us and his love is made complete in us.

1 *John* 4:12

This is how we know what love is: Jesus Christ laid down his life for us. And we ought to lay down our lives for our brothers.

1 *John* 3:16

Do not let this Book of the Law depart from your mouth; meditate on it day and night, so that you may be careful to do everything written in it. Then you will be prosperous and successful.

Joshua 1:8

Oh, how I love your law!
I mediate on it all day long.
Your commands make me wiser than my enemies,
for they are ever with me.
I have more insight than all my teachers,
for I meditate on your statues.

Psalm 119:97-99

May the words of my mouth and the
meditation of my heart
be pleasing in your sight,
O LORD, my Rock and my Redeemer.

Psalm 19:14

Let me understand the teaching of your
precepts, LORD;
then I will meditate on your wonders.
Psalm 119:27

I will meditate on all your works, O God,
and consider all your mighty deeds.
Psalm 77:12

Blessed is the man
who does not walk in the counsel
of the wicked
or stand in the way of sinners
or sit in the seat of mockers.
But his delight is in the law of the LORD,
and on his law he meditates day and night.
Psalm 1:1-2

I rise before dawn and cry for help;
I have put my hope in your word, LORD.
My eyes stay open through the watches of
the night,
that I may meditate on your promises.
Psalm 119:147-148

It was God who gave some to be apostles, some to be prophets, some to be evangelists, and some to be pastors and teachers, to prepare God's people for works of service, so that the body of Christ may be built up until we all reach unity in the faith and in the knowledge of the Son of God and become mature, attaining to the whole measure of the fullness of Christ.

Ephesians 4:11-13

God was reconciling the world to himself in Christ, not counting men's sins against them. And he has committed to us the message of reconciliation. We are therefore Christ's ambassadors, as though God were making his appeal through us.

2 *Corinthians* 5:19-20

Not that we are competent in ourselves to claim anything for ourselves, but our competence comes from God. He has made us competent as ministers of a new covenant—not of the letter but of the Spirit; for the letter kills, but the Spirit gives life.

2 Corinthians 3:5–6

Keep your head in all situations, endure hardship, do the work of an evangelist, discharge all the duties of your ministry.

2 Timothy 4:5

Serve wholeheartedly, as if you were serving the Lord, not men, because you know that the Lord will reward everyone for whatever good he does.

Ephesians 6:7–8

You alone are the LORD. You made the heavens, even the highest heavens, and all their starry host, the earth and all that is on it, the seas and all that is in them. You give life to everything, and the multitudes of heaven worship you.

Nehemiah 9:6

God has made everything beautiful in its time. He has also set eternity in the hearts of men; yet they cannot fathom what God has done from beginning to end.

Ecclesiastes 3:11

In the beginning you laid the foundations of
the earth, O God,
and the heavens are the work of your hands.

Psalm 102:25

The heavens declare the glory of God;
the skies proclaim the work of his hands.

Psalm 19:1

God created man in his own image,
in the image of God he created him;
male and female he created them. ...
Then God said, "I give you every seed-bearing plant on the face of the whole earth and every tree that has fruit with seed in it. They will be yours for food. And to all the beasts of the earth and all the birds of the air and all the creatures that move on the ground—everything that has the breath of life in it—I give every green plant for food." And it was so.

Genesis 1:27, 29-30

The LORD will indeed give what is good,
and our land will yield its harvest.

Psalm 85:12

To all who received him, to those who believed in his name, he gave the right to become children of God—children born not of natural descent, nor of human decision or a husband's will, but born of God.

John 1:12-13

God saved us, not because of righteous things we had done, but because of his mercy. He saved us through the washing of rebirth and renewal by the Holy Spirit.

Titus 3:5

If anyone is in Christ, he is a new creation; the old has gone, the new has come!

2 *Corinthians* 5:17

Jesus said, "Flesh gives birth to flesh, but the Spirit gives birth to spirit."

John 3:6

Do not lie to each other, since you have taken off your old self with its practices and have put on the new self, which is being renewed in knowledge in the image of its Creator.

Colossians 3:9-10

Every good and perfect gift is from above, coming down from the Father of the heavenly lights, who does not change like shifting shadows. He chose to give us birth through the word of truth, that we might be a kind of first fruits of all he created.

James 1:17-18

In his great mercy God has given us new birth into a living hope through the resurrection of Jesus Christ from the dead.

1 *Peter* 1:3

Jesus said, "If you obey my commands, you will remain in my love, just as I have obeyed my Father's commands and remain in his love. I have told you this so that my joy may be in you and that your joy may be complete."

John 15:10-11

It is the LORD your God you must follow, and him you must revere. Keep his commands and obey him; serve him and hold fast to him.

Deuteronomy 13:4

It is not those who hear the law who are righteous in God's sight, but it is those who obey the law who will be declared righteous.

Romans 2:13

If anyone obeys his word, God's love is truly made complete in him. This is how we know we are in him: Whoever claims to live in him must walk as Jesus did.

1 John 2:5

Jesus said, "Blessed rather are those who hear the word of God and obey it."

Luke 11:28

Jesus said, "Everyone who hears these words of mine and puts them into practice is like a wise man who built his house on the rock. The rain came down, the streams rose, and the winds blew and beat against that house; yet it did not fall, because it had its foundation on the rock."

Matthew 7:24-25

To obey is better than sacrifice,
and to heed is better than the fat of rams.

1 Samuel 15:22

Be patient, then, brothers, until the Lord's coming. See how the farmer waits for the land to yield its valuable crop and how patient he is for the autumn and spring rains. You too, be patient and stand firm, because the Lord's coming is near.

James 5:7-8

The end of a matter is better than its beginning,
and patience is better than pride.

Ecclesiastes 7:8

Be joyful in hope, patient in affliction, faithful in prayer.

Romans 12:12

I was shown mercy so that in me, the worst of sinners, Christ Jesus might display his unlimited patience as an example for those who would believe on him and receive eternal life.

1 Timothy 1:16

We pray this in order that you may live a life worthy of the Lord and may please him in every way: bearing fruit in every good work, growing in the knowledge of God, being strengthened with all power according to his glorious might so that you may have great endurance and patience.

Colossians 1:10-11

A patient man has great understanding.

Proverbs 14:29

The Lord is not slow in keeping his promise, as some understand slowness. He is patient with you, not wanting anyone to perish, but everyone to come to repentance.

2 *Peter* 3:9

Let us not become weary in doing good, for at the proper time we will reap a harvest if we do not give up.

Galatians 6:9

The LORD blesses his people with peace.

Psalm 29:11

Since we have been justified through faith, we have peace with God through our Lord Jesus Christ.

Romans 5:1

Aim for perfection, listen to my appeal, be of one mind, live in peace. And the God of love and peace will be with you.

2 *Corinthians* 13:11

The mind controlled by the Spirit is life and peace.

Romans 8:6

Do not be anxious about anything, but in everything, by prayer and petition, with thanksgiving, present your requests to God. And the peace of God, which transcends all understanding, will guard your hearts and your minds in Christ Jesus.

Philippians 4:6-7

Consider the blameless, observe the upright;
there is a future for the man of peace.

Psalm 37:37

Jesus said, "Blessed are the peacemakers,
for they will be called sons of God.

Matthew 5:9

Jesus said, "Peace I leave with you; my peace I give you. I do not give to you as the world gives. Do not let your hearts be troubled and do not be afraid."

John 14:27

I will lie down and sleep in peace,
for you alone, O LORD,
make me dwell in safety.

Psalm 4:8

How beautiful are the feet of those who bring good news!

Romans 10:15

Glory, honor and peace for everyone who does good: first for the Jew, then for the Gentile. For God does not show favoritism.

Romans 2:10-11

Great peace have they that love your law, LORD,
and nothing can make them stumble.

Psalm 119:165

You will keep in perfect peace
him whose mind is steadfast,
because he trust in you, LORD.

Isaiah 26:3

Peacemakers who sow in peace raise a harvest of righteousness.

James 3:18

When a man's ways are pleasing to the LORD,
he makes even his enemies live at peace
with him.

Proverbs 16:7

The kingdom of God is not a matter of eating and drinking, but of righteousness, peace and joy in the Holy Spirit, because anyone who serves Christ in this way is pleasing to God and approved by men. Let us therefore make every effort to do what leads to peace and to mutual edification.

Romans 14:17-19

Let the peace of Christ rule in your hearts, since as members of one body you were called to peace.

Colossians 3:15

The God of peace will soon crush Satan under your feet.

Romans 16:20

Grace and peace be yours in abundance through the knowledge of God and of Jesus our Lord.

2 *Peter* 1:2

The testing of your faith develops perseverance. Perseverance must finish its work so that you may be mature and complete, not lacking anything.

James 1:3-4

Let us not become weary in doing good, for at the proper time we will reap a harvest if we do not give up.

Galatians 6:9

To those who by persistence in doing good seek glory, honor and immortality, he will give eternal life.

Romans 2:7

My steps have held to your paths, O LORD;
my feet have not slipped.

Psalm 17:5

We also rejoice in our sufferings, because we know that suffering produces perseverance; perseverance, character; and character, hope.

Romans 5:3-4

You need to persevere so that when you have done the will of God, you will receive what he has promised.

Hebrews 10:36

We consider blessed those who have persevered. You have heard of Job's perseverance and have seen what the Lord finally brought about. The Lord is full of compassion and mercy.

James 5:11

Blessed is the man who perseveres under trial, because when he has stood the test, he will receive the crown of life that God has promised to those who love him.

James 1:12

May the Lord direct your hearts into God's love and Christ's perseverance.

2 *Thessalonians* 3:5

The Lord said, "Hold on to what you have until I come. To him who overcomes and does my will to the end, I will give authority over the nations."

Revelation 2:25-26

When God gives any man wealth and possessions, and enables him to enjoy them, to accept his lot and be happy in his work—this is a gift of God.

Ecclesiastes 5:19

Jesus said, "Watch out! Be on your guard against all kinds of greed; a man's life does not consist in the abundance of his possessions."

Luke 12:15

You sympathized with those in prison and joyfully accepted the confiscation of your property, because you knew that you yourselves had better and lasting possessions.

Hebrews 10:34

If I give all I possess to the poor and surrender my body to the flames, but have not love, I gain nothing.

1 Corinthians 13:3

As servants of God we commend ourselves in every way: ... poor, yet making many rich; having nothing, and yet possessing everything.

2 Corinthians 6:4, 10

A scroll of remembrance was written in God's presence concerning those who feared the LORD and honored his name. "They will be mine," says the LORD Almighty, "in the day when I make up my treasured possession. I will spare them, just as in compassion a man spares his son who serves him."

Malachi 3:16-17

"Ask of me,
and I will make the nations your inheritance,
the ends of the earth your possession."

Psalm 2:8

Jesus said to me, "My grace is sufficient for you, for my power is made perfect in weakness." Therefore I will boast all the more gladly about my weaknesses, so that Christ's power may rest on me.

2 Corinthians 12:9

I pray that out of God's glorious riches he may strengthen you with power through his Spirit in your inner being.

Ephesians 3:16

God gives strength to the weary
and increases the power of the weak.

Isaiah 40:29

God did not give us a spirit of timidity, but a spirit of power, of love and of self-discipline.

2 Timothy 1:7

May the God of hope fill you with all joy and peace as you trust in him, so that you may overflow with hope by the power of the Holy Spirit.

Romans 15:13

Praise God in his sanctuary;
  praise him in his mighty heavens.
Praise him for his acts of power;
  praise him for his surpassing greatness.

Psalm 150:1-2

Even when I am old and gray,
  do not forsake me, O God,
till I declare your power to the next generation,
  your might to all who are to come.

Psalm 71:18

I am not ashamed of the gospel, because it is the power of God for the salvation of everyone who believes.

Romans 1:16

The heavens praise your wonders, O LORD,
your faithfulness too, in the assembly of the holy ones.
For who in the skies above can compare with the LORD?
Who is like the LORD among the heavenly beings?
In the council of the holy ones God is greatly feared;
he is more awesome than all who surround him.
O LORD God Almighty, who is like you?
You are mighty, O LORD, and your faithfulness surrounds you.

Psalm 89:5-8

The LORD takes delight in his people;
he crowns the humble with salvation.
Let the saints rejoice in this honor
and sing for joy on their beds.
May the praise of God be in their mouths.

Psalm 149:4-6

I urge, you, brothers, in view of God's mercy, to offer your bodies as living sacrifices, holy and pleasing to God—this is your spiritual act of worship.

Romans 12:1

I will praise you, O Lord my God, with all
 my heart;
 I will glorify your name forever.
For great is your love toward me;
 you have delivered me from the depths of
 the grave.

Psalm 86:12-13

The LORD lives! Praise be to my Rock!
 Exalted be God, the Rock, my Savior!

2 *Samuel* 22:47

Great is the LORD and most worthy of praise;
 he is to be feared above all gods.

1 *Chronicles* 16:25

"If my people, who are called by my name, will humble themselves and pray and seek my face and turn from their wicked ways, then will I hear from heaven and will forgive their sin and will heal their land," declares the LORD.

2 Chronicles 7:14

Jesus said, "When you stand praying, if you hold anything against anyone, forgive him, so that your Father in heaven may forgive you your sins."

Mark 11:25

"You will call upon me and come and pray to me, and I will listen to you. You will seek me and find me when you seek me with all your heart," says the LORD.

Jeremiah 29:12-13

The eyes of the Lord are on the righteous and his ears are attentive to their prayers.

1 Peter 3:12

Jesus said, "When you pray go into your room, close the door and pray to your Father, who is unseen. Then your Father, who sees what is done in secret, will reward you."

Matthew 6:6

Pray in the Spirit on all occasions with all kinds of prayers and requests. With this in mind, be alert and always keep on praying for all the saints.

Ephesians 6:18

The prayer offered in faith will make the sick person well; the Lord will raise him up. If he has sinned, he will be forgiven.

James 5:15

The LORD is far from the wicked
but he hears the prayer of the righteous.

Proverbs 15:29

Let everyone who is godly pray to you, LORD,
while you may be found;
surely when the mighty waters rise,
they will not reach him.

Psalm 32:6

The LORD has heard my cry for mercy;
the LORD accepts my prayer.

Psalm 6:9

We have not stopped praying for you and asking God to fill you with the knowledge of his will through all spiritual wisdom and understanding.

Colossians 1:9

"Before they call I will answer;
while they are still speaking I will hear,"
says the LORD.

Isaiah 65:24

Jesus said, "I tell you the truth, my Father will give you whatever you ask in my name. Until now you have not asked for anything in my name. Ask and you will receive, and your joy will be complete."

John 16:23-24

The Spirit helps us in our weakness. We do not know what we ought to pray for, but he Spirit himself intercedes for us with groans that words cannot express.

Romans 8:26

Do not be anxious about anything, but in everything, by prayer and petition, with thanksgiving, present your requests to God. And the peace of God, which transcends all understanding, will guard your hearts and your minds in Christ Jesus.

Philippians 4:6-7

Jesus said, "If anyone would come after me, he must deny himself and take up his cross and follow me. For whoever wants to save his life will lose it, but whoever loses his life for me will find it."

Matthew 16:24–25

Imitate those who through faith and patience inherit what has been promised.

Hebrews 6:12

Jesus said, "Do not worry, saying, 'What shall we eat?' or 'What shall we drink?' or 'What shall we wear?' ... Seek first God's kingdom and his righteousness, and all these things will be given to you as well."

Matthew 6:31, 33

He who pursues righteousness and love
finds life, prosperity and honor.

Proverbs 21:21

Let us fix our eyes on Jesus, the author and perfecter of our faith, who for the joy set before him endured the cross, scorning its shame, and sat down at the right hand of the throne of God.

Hebrews 12:2

Look to the LORD and his strength;
    seek his face always.
Remember the wonders he has done,
    his miracles, and the judgments he pronounced.

1 *Chronicles* 16:11–12

We fix our eyes not on what is seen, but on what is unseen. For what is seen is temporary, but what is unseen is eternal.

2 *Corinthians* 4:18

My soul clings to you;
    your right hand upholds me, LORD.

Psalm 63:8

The Lord is faithful, and he will strengthen and protect you from the evil one.

2 Thessalonians 3:3

"Because he loves me," says the LORD,
"I will rescue him;
I will protect him, for he acknowledges my name.
He will call upon me, and I will answer him;
I will be with him in trouble,
I will deliver him and honor him."

Psalm 91:14-15

The LORD loves the just
and will not forsake his faithful ones.
They will be protected forever.

Psalm 37:28

The LORD watches over all who love him.

Psalm 145:20

The eternal God is your refuge,
and underneath are the everlasting arms.

Deuteronomy 33:27

If you make the Most High your dwelling—
even the LORD, who is my refuge—
then no harm will befall you,
no disaster will come near your tent.
For he will command his angels concerning you
to guard you in all your ways.

Psalm 91:9-11

The LORD will keep you from all harm—
he will watch over your life;
the LORD will watch over your coming and going
both now and forevermore.

Psalm 121:7-8

"No weapon forged against you will prevail,
and you will refute every tongue that
accuses you.
This is the heritage of the servants of the LORD,
and this is their vindication from me,"
declares the LORD.

Isaiah 54:17

God is able to make all grace abound to you, so that in all things at all times, having all that you need, you will abound in every good work.

2 Corinthians 9:8

Jesus said, "Why do you worry about clothes? See how the lilies of the field grow. They do not labor or spin. Yet I tell you that not even Solomon in all his splendor was dressed like one of these. If that is how God clothes the grass of the field, which is here today and tomorrow is thrown into the fire, will he not much more clothe you, O you of little faith? So do not worry, saying, 'What shall we eat?' or 'What shall we drink?' or 'What shall we wear?' For the pagans run after all these things, and your heavenly Father knows that you need them."

Matthew 6:28-32

My God will meet all your needs according to his glorious riches in Christ Jesus.

Philippians 4:19

God has shown kindness by giving you rain from heaven and crops in their seasons; he provides you with plenty of food and fills your hearts with joy.

Acts 14:17

Command those who are rich in this present world not to be arrogant nor to put their hope in wealth, which is so uncertain, but to put their hope in God, who richly provides us with everything for our enjoyment.

1 *Timothy* 6:17

The LORD will guide you always;
he will satisfy your needs in a sun-scorched
land
and will strengthen your frame.
You will be like a well-watered garden,
like a spring whose waters never fail.

Isaiah 58:11

Come near to God and he will come near to you. ... Humble yourselves before the Lord, and he will lift you up.

James 4:8, 10

Don't let anyone look down on you because you are young, but set an example for the believers in speech, in life, in love, in faith and in purity.

1 *Timothy* 4:12

How can a young man keep his way pure?
By living according to your word. ...
I have hidden your word in my heart
that I might not sin against you, LORD.

Psalm 119:9, 11

He who loves a pure heart and whose speech is gracious
will have the king for a friend.

Proverbs 22:11

The wisdom that comes from heaven is first of all pure; then peace-loving, considerate, submissive, fill of mercy and good fruit, impartial and sincere. Peacemakers who sow in peace raise a harvest of righteousness.

James 3:17-18

Jesus said, "Blessed are the pure in heart,
for they will see God."

Matthew 5:8

If we walk in the light, as he is in the light, we have fellowship with one another, and the blood of Jesus, his Son, purifies us from all sin.

1 *John* 1:7

To the pure you show yourself pure.

Psalm 18:26

The LORD will fulfill his purpose for me;
your love, O LORD, endures forever—
do not abandon the works of your hands.

Psalm 138:8

We know that in all things God works for the good of those who love him, who have been called according to his purpose.

Romans 8:28

We are God's workmanship, created in Christ Jesus to do good works, which God prepared in advance for us to do.

Ephesians 2:10

Do not conform any longer to the pattern of this world, but be transformed by the renewing of your mind. Then you will be able to test and approve what God's will is—his good, pleasing and perfect will.

Romans 12:2

Make it your ambition to lead a quiet life, mind your own business and work with yo hands, just as we told you.

1 Thessalonians 4:11

I say to myself, "The LORD is my portion;
therefore I will wait for him."
The LORD is good to those whose hope
is in him,
to the one who seeks him;
it is good to wait quietly
for the salvation of the LORD.

Lamentations 3:24-26

I have stilled and quieted my soul;
like a weaned child with its mother,
like a weaned child is my soul within me.

Psalm 131:2

The LORD will fight for you; you need only to be still.

Exodus 14:14

All have sinned and fall short of the glory of God, and are justified freely by his grace through the redemption that came by Christ Jesus.

Romans 3:23-24

We ourselves, who have the firstfruits of the Spirit, groan inwardly as we wait eagerly for our adoption as sons, the redemption of our bodies.

Romans 8:23

In Christ, we have redemption through his blood, the forgiveness of sins, in accordance with the riches of God's grace that he lavished on us with all wisdom and understanding.

Ephesians 1:7-8

God has rescued us from the dominion of darkness and brought us into the kingdom of the Son he loves, in whom we have redemption, the forgiveness of sins.

Colossians 1:13-14

"Everyone who confesses the name of the Lord must turn away from wickedness." ... If a man cleanses himself from [wickedness], he will be an instrument for noble purposes, made holy, useful to the Master and prepared to do any good work.

2 Timothy 2:19, 21

We constantly pray for you, that our God may count you worthy of his calling, and that by his power he may fulfill every good purpose of yours and every act prompted by your faith.

2 Thessalonians 1:11

Because God wanted to make the unchanging nature of his purpose very clear to the heirs of what was promised, he confirmed it with an oath. God did this so that ... we who have fled to take hold of the hope offered to us may be greatly encouraged.

Hebrews 6:17-18

[Your beauty] should be that of your inner self, the unfading beauty of a gentle and quiet spirit, which is of great worth in God's sight.

1 Peter 3:4

The effect of righteousness will be quietness and confidence forever.

Isaiah 32:17

I urge, then, first of all, that requests, prayers, intercession and thanksgiving be made for everyone—for kings and all those in authority, that we may live peaceful and quiet lives in all godliness and holiness. This is good, and pleases God our Savior, who wants all men to be saved and to come to a knowledge of the truth.

1 Timothy 2:1-4

God redeemed us in order that the blessing given to Abraham might come to the Gentiles through Christ Jesus.

Galatians 3:14

It was not with perishable things such as silver or gold that you were redeemed from the empty way of life handed down to you from your forefathers, but with the precious blood of Christ, a lamb without blemish or defect.

1 Peter 1:18–19

Put your hope in the LORD,
for with the LORD is unfailing love
and with him is full redemption.

Psalm 130:7

Praise the LORD. ...
He provided redemption for his people;
he ordained his covenant forever—
holy and awesome is his name.

Psalm 111:1, 9

See to it that no one misses the grace of God and that no bitter root grows up to cause trouble and defile many.

Hebrews 12:15

God was pleased to have all his fullness dwell in Christ, and through him to reconcile to himself all things, whether things on earth or things in heaven, by making peace through his blood, shed on the cross.

Colossians 1:19-20

If, when we were God's enemies, we were reconciled to him through the death of his Son, how much more, having been reconciled, shall we be saved through his life! Not only is this so, but we also rejoice in God through our Lord Jesus Christ, through whom we have now received reconciliation.

Romans 5:10-11

If anyone is in Christ, he is a new creation; the old has gone, the new has come! All this is from God, who reconciled us to himself through Christ and gave us the ministry of reconciliation: that God was reconciling the world to himself in Christ, not counting men's sins against them. And he has committed to us the message of reconciliation. We are therefore Christ's ambassadors, as though God were making his appeal through us. We implore you on Christ's behalf: Be reconciled to God.

2 *Corinthians* 5:17-20

Jesus said, "When you stand praying, if you hold anything against anyone, forgive him, so that your Father in heaven may forgive you your sins."

Mark 11:25

Do not hide your face from me,
do not turn your servant away in anger;
you have been my helper.
Do not reject me or forsake me,
O God my Savior.
Though my father and mother forsake me,
the LORD will receive me.

Psalm 27:9-10

Jesus said, "All that the Father gives me will come to me, and whoever comes to me I will never drive away. For I have come down from heaven not to do my will but to do the will of him who sent me. And this is the will of him who sent me, that I shall lose none of all that he has given me, but raise them up at the last day."

John 6:37-39

The LORD will not reject his people;
he will never forsake his inheritance.

Psalm 94:14

Those who know your name will trust in you,
for you, LORD, have never forsaken those
who seek you.

Psalm 9:10

Jesus said, "He who listens to you listens to me; he who rejects you rejects me; but he who rejects me rejects him who sent me."

Luke 10:16

As you come to him, the living Stone—rejected by men but chosen by God and precious to him—you also, like living stones, are being built into a spiritual house to be a holy priesthood, offering spiritual sacrifices acceptable to God through Jesus Christ.

1 Peter 2:4-5

Repent then, and turn to God, so that your sins may be wiped out, that times of refreshing may come from the Lord.

Acts 3:19

Jesus said, "I tell you that in the same way there will be more rejoicing in heaven over one sinner who repents than over ninety-nine righteous persons who do not need to repent."

Luke 15:7

The Lord is not slow in keeping his promise, as some understand slowness. He is patient with you, not wanting anyone to perish, but everyone to come to repentance.

2 *Peter* 3:9

Godly sorrow brings repentance that leads to salvation and leaves no regret.

2 *Corinthians* 7:10

Peter replied, "Repent and be baptized, every one of you, in the name of Jesus Christ for the forgiveness of your sins. And you will receive the gift of the Holy Spirit."

Acts 2:38

"If my people, who are called by my name, will humble themselves and pray and seek my face and turn from their wicked ways, then will I hear from heaven and will forgive their sin and will heal their land," says the LORD.

2 *Chronicles* 7:14

Jesus said, "It is not the healthy who need a doctor, but the sick. I have not come to call the righteous, but sinners to repentance."

Luke 5:31-32

This is what the Sovereign LORD, the Holy One of Israel, says:

"In repentance and rest is your salvation,
in quietness and trust is your strength."

Isaiah 30:15

Let the wicked forsake his way
and the evil man his thoughts.
Let him turn to the LORD, and he will have
mercy on him,
and to our God, for he will freely pardon.

Isaiah 55:7

"If a wicked man turns away from all the sins he has committed and keeps all my decrees and does what is just and right, he will surely live; he will not die. None of the offenses he has committed will be remembered against him. Because of the righteous things he has done, he will live," says the LORD.

Ezekiel 18:21-22

These are the words of the Amen, the faithful and true witness, the ruler of God's creation. ... "Those whom I love I rebuke and discipline. So be earnest, and repent."

Revelation 3:14, 19

Jesus said, "If your brother sins, rebuke him, and if he repents, forgive him. If he sins against you seven times in a day, and seven times comes back to you and says, 'I repent,' forgive him."

Luke 17:3-4

Whenever anyone turns to the Lord, the veil is taken away. Now the Lord is the Spirit, and where the Spirit of the Lord is, there is freedom.

2 *Corinthians* 3:16-17

Jesus said, "Come to me, all you who are weary and burdened, and I will give you rest. Take my yoke upon you and learn from me, for I am gentle and humble in heart, and you will find rest for your souls. For my yoke is easy and my burden is light."

Matthew 11:28-30

There remains a Sabbath-rest for the people of God; for anyone who enters God's rest also rests from his own work, just as God did from his. Let us, therefore, make every effort to enter that rest.

Hebrews 4:9-11

"I will refresh the weary and satisfy the faint," says the LORD.

Jeremiah 31:25

Be at rest once more, O my soul,
for the LORD has been good to you.

Psalm 116:7

My soul finds rest in God alone;
my salvation comes from him.
He alone is my rock and my salvation;
he is my fortress, I will never be shaken.

Psalm 62:1-2

He who dwells in the shelter of the Most High
will rest in the shadow of the Almighty.

Psalm 91:1

The LORD is my shepherd, I shall not
be in want.
He makes me lie down in green pastures,
he leads me beside quiet waters,
he restores my soul.
He guides me in paths of righteousness
for his name's sake.

Psalm 23:1-3

I will repay you for the years the locusts have eaten—the great locust and the young locust, the other locusts and the locust swarm—my great army that I sent among you. You will have plenty to eat, until you are full, and you will praise the name of the LORD your God, who has worked wonders for you; never again will my people be shamed.

Joel 2:25-26

The God of all grace, who called you to his eternal glory in Christ, after you have suffered a little while, will himself restore you and make you strong, firm and steadfast.

1 Peter 5:10

Restore us, O God;
make your face shine upon us,
that we may be saved.

Psalm 80:3

In Christ Jesus you who once were far away have been brought near through the blood of Christ.

Ephesians 2:13

"I will search for the lost and bring back the strays. I will bind up the injured and strengthen the weak," says the LORD.

Ezekiel 34:16

"I will restore you to health
    and heal your wounds," declares the LORD,
"because you are called an outcast,
    Zion for whom no one cares."

Jeremiah 30:17

Though you have made me see troubles,
        many and bitter,
    you will restore my life again;
from the depths of the earth
    you will again bring me up.
You will increase my honor
    and comfort me once again.

Psalm 71:20-21

Whatever you do, work at it with all your heart, as working for the Lord, not for men, since you know that you will receive an inheritance from the Lord as a reward. It is the Lord Christ you a re serving.

Colossians 3:23-24

Jesus said, "Behold, I am coming soon! My reward is with me, and I will give to everyone according to what he has done."

Revelation 22:12

Jesus said, "When you pray go into your room, close the door and pray to your Father, who is unseen. Then your Father, who sees what is done in secret, will reward you."

Matthew 6:6

You know that the Lord will reward everyone for whatever good he does.

Ephesians 6:8

Jesus said, "Love your enemies, do good to them, and lend to them without expecting to get anything back. Then your reward will be great, and you will be sons of the Most High."

Luke 6:35

Jesus said, "If anyone gives even a cup of cold water to one of these little ones because he is my disciple, I tell you the truth, he will certainly not lose his reward."

Matthew 10:42

"I the LORD search the heart
    and examine the mind,
to reward a man according to his conduct,
    according to what his deeds deserve."

Jeremiah 17:10

Fire will test the quality of each man's work. If what he has built survives, he will receive his reward.

1 Corinthians 3:13-14

The fruit of the righteous is a tree of life,
and he who wins souls is wise.

Proverbs 11:30

The eyes of the Lord are on the righteous and
his ears are attentive to their prayer.

1 *Peter* 3:12

The path of the righteous is like the first
gleam of dawn,
shining ever brighter till the full light of day.

Proverbs 4:18

Jesus said, "Blessed are those who hunger and
thirst for righteousness,
for they will be filled."

Matthew 5:6

God does not take his eyes off the righteous;
he enthrones them with kings and exalts
them forever.

Job 36:7

In the way of righteousness there is life;
along that path is immortality.

Proverbs 12:28

The prayer of a righteous man is powerful and effective.

James 5:16

Do not let anyone lead you astray. He who does what is right is righteous, just as God is righteous.

1 John 3:7

Judgment will again be founded on righteousness,
and all the upright in heart will follow it.

Psalm 94:14

Sow for yourselves righteousness,
reap the fruit of unfailing love,
and break up your unplowed ground;
for it is time to seek the LORD,
until he comes
and showers righteousness on you.

Hosea 10:12

The mouth of the righteous man utters wisdom,
and his tongue speaks what is just.
The law of his God is in his heart;
his feet do not slip.

Psalm 37:30-31

I urge, you, brothers, in view of God's mercy, to offer your bodies as living sacrifices, holy and pleasing to God—this is your spiritual act of worship.

Romans 12:1

Through Jesus ... let us continually offer to God a sacrifice of praise—the fruit of lips that confess his name. Do not forget to do good and to sharewith others, for with such sacrifices God is pleased.

Hebrews 13:15-16

As you come to him, the living Stone—rejected by men but chosen by God and precious to him—you also, like living stones, are being built into a spiritual house to be a holy priesthood, offering spiritual sacrifices acceptable to God through Jesus Christ.

1 *Peter* 2:4-5

O LORD, open my lips,
and my mouth will declare your praise.
You do not delight in sacrifice, or I would
bring it;
you do not take pleasure in burnt offerings.
The sacrifices of God are a broken spirit;
a broken and contrite heart,
O God, you will not despise.

Psalm 51:15-17

I will sacrifice a freewill offering to you;
I will praise your name, O LORD,
for it is good.
For he has delivered me from all my troubles,
and my eyes have looked in triumph on
my foes.

Psalm 54:6-7

To do what is right and just
is more acceptable to the LORD than sacrifice.

Proverbs 21:3

The hour has come for you to wake up from your slumber, because our salvation is nearer now than when we first believed. The night is nearly over; the day is almost here. So let us put aside the deeds of darkness and put on the armor of light.

Romans 13:11-12

Like newborn babies, crave pure spiritual milk, so that by it you may grow up in your salvation, now that you have tasted that the Lord is good.

1 *Peter* 2:2-3

Continue to work out your salvation with fear and trembling, for it is God who works in you to will and to act according to his good purpose.

Philippians 2:12-13

Once made perfect, Jesus became the source of eternal salvation for all who obey him.

Hebrews 5:9

Now is the time of God's favor, now is the day of salvation.

2 *Corinthians* 6:2

Christ was sacrificed once to take away the sins of many people; and he will appear a second time, not to bear sin, but to bring salvation to those who are waiting for him.

Hebrews 9:28

God did not appoint us to suffer wrath but to receive salvation through our Lord Jesus Christ. He died for us so that, whether we are awake or asleep, we may live together with him.

1 *Thessalonians* 5:9-10

You open your hand
and satisfy the desires of every living thing,
LORD.

Psalm 145:16

The LORD will guide you always;
he will satisfy your needs in a sun-scorched land
and will strengthen your frame.
You will be like a well-watered garden,
like a spring whose waters never fail.

Isaiah 58:11

A man can do nothing better than to eat and drink and find satisfaction in his work. This too, I see, is from the hand of God.

Ecclesiastes 2:24

Jesus said, "Blessed are you who hunger now,
for you will be satisfied.

Luke 6:21

"With long life will I satisfy him
and show him my salvation," says the LORD.

Psalm 91:16

"I will refresh the weary and satisfy the faint,"
says the LORD.

Jeremiah 31:25

My soul will be satisfied as with the richest of foods;
with singing lips my mouth will praise you, LORD.

Psalm 63:5

"Come all you who are thirsty,
come to the waters;
and you who have no money,
come, buy and eat!
Come, buy wine and milk
without money and without cost.
Why spend money on what is not bread,
and your labor on what does not satisfy?
Listen, listen to me, and eat what is good,
and your soul will delight in the richest of fare," says the LORD.

Isaiah 55:1-2

The LORD satisfies your desires with good things
so that your youth is renewed like the eagle's.

Psalm 103:5

Everything that was written in the past was written to teach us, so that through endurance and the encouragement of the Scriptures we might have hope.

Romans 15:4

Continue in what you have learned and have become convinced of, because you know those from whom you learned it, and how from infancy you have known the holy Scriptures, which are able to make you wise for salvation through faith in Christ Jesus.

2 *Timothy* 3:14–15

The word of God is living and active. Sharper than any double-edged sword, it penetrates even to dividing soul and spirit, joints and marrow; it judges the thoughts and attitudes of the heart.

Hebrews 4:12

The Scriptures declares that the whole world is a prisoner of sin, so that what was promised, being given through faith in Jesus Christ, might be given to those who believe.

Galatians 3:22

All Scripture is God-breathed and is useful for teaching, rebuking, correcting and training in righteousness, so that the man of God may be thoroughly equipped for every good work.

2 *Timothy* 3:16-17

Jesus opened [the disciples'] minds so they could understand the Scriptures. He told them, "This is what is written: The Christ will suffer and rise from the dead on the third day, and repentance and forgiveness of sins will be preached in his name to all nations."

Luke 24:45-47

Let the beloved of the LORD rest secure in him,
for he shields him all day long
and the one the LORD loves rests between
his shoulders.

Deuteronomy 33:12

"My people will live in peaceful dwelling places,
in secure homes,
in undisturbed places of rest.
Though hail flattens the forest
and the city is leveled completely,
how blessed you will be," says the LORD.

Isaiah 32:18-20

"Do not take advantage of each other, but fear your God. I am the LORD your God. Follow my decrees and be careful to obey my laws, and you will live safely in the land. Then the land will yield its fruit, and you will eat your fill and live there in safety."

Leviticus 25:17-19

The name of the LORD is a strong tower;
the righteous run to it and are safe.

Proverbs 18:10

I will lie down and sleep in peace,
for you alone, O LORD,
make me dwell in safety.

Psalm 4:8

A righteous man will be remembered forever.
He will have no fear of bad news;
his heart is steadfast, trusting in the LORD.
His heart is secure, he will have no fear;
in the end he will look in triumph on his foes.

Psalm 112:6-8

I have set the LORD always before me.
Because he is at my right hand,
I will not be shaken.
Therefore my heart is glad and my tongue rejoices;
my body also will rest secure.

Psalm 16:8-9

Seek the LORD while he may be found;
call on him while he is near.
Let the wicked forsake his way
and the evil man his thoughts.
Let him turn to the LORD, and he will have
mercy on him,
and to our God, for he will freely pardon.

Isaiah 55:6-7

"You will call upon me and come and pray to me, and I will listen to you. You will seek me and find me when you seek me with all your heart. I will be found by you," declares the LORD.

Jeremiah 29:12-14

Let the hearts of those who seek the LORD
rejoice.
Look to the LORD and his strength;
seek his face always.

Psalm 105:3-4

Jesus said, "Ask and it will be given to you; seek and you will find; knock and the door will be opened to you. For everyone who asks receives; he who seeks finds; and to him who knocks, the door will be opened."

Luke 11:9-10

Without faith it is impossible to please God, because anyone who comes to him must believe that he exists and that he rewards those who earnestly seek him.

Hebrews 11:6

Sow for yourselves righteousness,
    reap the fruit of unfailing love,
and break up your unplowed ground;
    for it is time to seek the LORD,
until he comes
    and showers righteousness on you.

Hosea 10:12

Live self-controlled, upright and godly lives in this present age, while we wait for the blessed hope—the glorious appearance of our great God and Savior, Jesus Christ.

Titus 2:12-13

Since we belong to the day, let us be self-controlled, putting on faith and love as a breastplate, and the hope of salvation as a helmet.

1 *Thessalonians* 5:8

Prepare your minds for action; be self-controlled, set your hope fully on the grace to be given you when Jesus Christ is revealed.

1 *Peter* 1:13

Be self-controlled and alert. Your enemy the devil prowls around like a roaring lion looking for someone to devour. Resist him, standing firm in the faith.

1 *Peter* 5:8-9

The end of all things is near. Therefore be clear minded and self-controlled so that you can pray.

1 Peter 4:7

No temptation has seized you except what is common to man. And God is faithful; he will not let you be tempted beyond that you can bear. But when you are tempted, he will also provide a way out so that you can stand up under it.

1 Corinthians 10:13

Only be careful, and watch yourselves closely so that you do not forget the things your eyes have seen or let them slip from your heart as long as you live. Teach them to your children and to their children after them.

Deuteronomy 4:9

God chose us in him before the creation of the world to be holy and blameless in his sight. In love he predestined us to be adopted as his sons through Jesus Christ, in accordance with his pleasure and will—to the praise of his glorious grace, which he has freely given us in the One he loves.

Ephesians 1:4-6

Know that the LORD is God.
It is he who made us, and we are his;
we are his people, the sheep of his pasture.

Psalm 100:3

"Before I formed you in the womb I knew you,
before you were born I set you apart,"
says the LORD.

Jeremiah 1:5

Do you not know that your body is a temple of the Holy Spirit, who is in you, whom you have received from God? You are not your own; you are bought at a price. Therefore honor God with your body.

1 Corinthians 6:19-20

You have put on the new self, which is being renewed in knowledge in the image of its Creator.

Colossians 3:10

Jesus said, "Are not two sparrows sold for a penny? Yet not one of them will fall to the ground apart from the will of your Father. And even the very hairs of your head are all numbered. So don't be afraid; you are worth more than many sparrows."

Matthew 10:29-31

Serve wholeheartedly, as if you were serving the Lord, not men, because you know that the Lord will reward everyone for whatever good he does.

Ephesians 6:7-8

Each one should use whatever gift he has received to serve others, faithfully administering God's grace in its various forms. If anyone speaks, he should do it as one speaking the very words of God. If anyone serves, he should do it with the strength God provides, so that in all things God may be praised through Jesus Christ.

1 Peter 4:10-11

Acknowledge the God of your father, and serve him with wholehearted devotion and with a willing mind, for the LORD searches every heart and understands every motive behind the thoughts.

1 Chronicles 28:9

Whatever you do, work at it with all your heart, as working for the Lord, not for men, since you know that you will receive an inheritance from the Lord as a reward. It is the Lord Christ you are serving.

Colossians 3:23-24

It was God who gave some to be apostles, some to be prophets, some to be evangelists, and some to be pastors and teachers, to prepare God's people for works of service, so that the body of Christ may be built up until we all reach unity in the faith and in the knowledge of the Son of God and become mature, attaining to the whole measure of the fullness of Christ.

Ephesians 4:11-13

Since we have a great priest over the house of God, let us draw near to God with a sincere heart in full assurance of faith, having our hearts sprinkled to cleanse us from a guilty conscience and having our bodies washed with pure water. Let us hold unswervingly to the hope we profess, for he who promised is faithful.

Hebrews 10:21–23

We do not peddle the word of God for profit. On the contrary, in Christ we speak before God with sincerity, like men sent from God.

2 *Corinthians* 2:17

Now that you have purified yourselves by obeying the truth so that you have sincere love for your brothers, love one another deeply, from the heart.

1 *Peter* 1:22

Love must be sincere. Hate what is evil, cling to what is good. Be devoted to one another in brotherly love. Honor one another above yourselves.

Romans 12:9-10

Obey your earthly masters in everything; and do it, not only when their eye is on you and to win their favor but with sincerity of heart and reverence for the Lord.

Colossians 3:22

Now this is our boast: Our conscience testifies that we have conducted ourselves in the world, and especially in our relations with you, in the holiness and sincerity that are from God. We have done so not according to worldly wisdom but according to God's grace.

2 *Corinthians* 1:12

Whoever would love life and see good days must keep his tongue from evil and his lips from deceitful speech.

1 Peter 3:10

Let your conversation be always full of grace, seasoned with salt, so that you may know how to answer everyone.

Colossians 4:6

Don't let anyone look down on you because you are young, but set an example for the believers in speech, in life, in love, in faith and in purity.

1 Timothy 4:12

We all stumble in many ways. If anyone is never at fault in what he says, he is a perfect man, able to keep his whole body in check.

James 3:2

Speaking the truth in love, we will in all things grow up into him who is the Head, that is, Christ.

Ephesians 4:15

The tongue that brings healing is a tree of life,
but a deceitful tongue crushes the spirit.

Proverbs 15:4

The speech of the upright rescues them.

Proverbs 12:6

He who loves a pure heart and whose speech
is gracious
will have the king for a friend.

Proverbs 22:11

Pleasant words are a honeycomb,
sweet to the soul and healing to the bones.

Proverbs 16:24

The quiet words of the wise are more to
be heeded
than the shouts of a ruler of fools.

Ecclesiastes 9:17

He who guards his mouth and his tongue
keeps himself from calamity.

Proverbs 21:23

Great peace have they that love your law, LORD,
and nothing can make them stumble.

Psalm 119:165

If the LORD delights in a man's way,
he makes his steps firm;
though he stumble, he will not fall,
for the LORD upholds him with his hand.

Psalm 37:23-24

Whoever loves his brother lives in the light, and there is nothing in him to make him stumble.

1 John 2:10

To him who is able to keep you from falling and to present you before his glorious presence without fault and with great joy—too the only God our Savior be glory, majesty, power and authority, through Jesus Christ our Lord, before all ages, now and forever more! Amen.

Jude 1:24-25

I have set the LORD always before me.
Because he is at my right hand,
I will not be shaken.

Psalm 16:8

You, O LORD, have delivered my soul from death,
my eyes from tears,
my feet from stumbling,
that I may walk before the LORD
in the land of the living.

Psalm 116:8-9

My soul finds rest in God alone;
my salvation comes from him.
He alone is my rock and my salvation;
he is my fortress, I will never be shaken.

Psalm 62:1-2

The God of all grace, who called you to his eternal glory in Christ, after you have suffered a little while, will himself restore you and make you strong, firm and steadfast.

1 Peter 5:10

You do not lack any spiritual gift as you eagerly wait for our Lord Jesus Christ to be revealed. He will keep you strong to the end, so that you will be blameless on the day of our Lord Jesus Christ.

1 Corinthians 1:7-8

The LORD gives strength to his people.

Psalm 29:11

I can do everything through Christ who gives me strength.

Philippians 4:13

I pray that out of God's glorious riches he may strengthen you with power through his Spirit in your inner being.

Ephesians 3:16

"Do not fear, for I am with you;
do not be dismayed, for I am your God.
I will strengthen you and help you;
I will uphold you with my righteous right hand."

Isaiah 41:10

My flesh and my heart may fail,
but God is the strength of my heart
and my portion forever.

Psalm 73:26

The LORD gives strength to the weary
and increases the power of the weak.

Isaiah 40:29

May God strengthen your hearts so that you will be blameless and holy in the presence of our God and Father when our Lord Jesus comes with all his holy ones.

1 Thessalonians 3:13

God is our refuge and strength,
an ever-present help in trouble.

Psalm 46:1

Those who hope in the LORD
will renew their strength.
They will soar on wings like eagles;
they will run and not grow weary,
they will walk and not be faint.

Isaiah 40:31

The LORD is my strength and my song;
he has become my salvation.
He is my God, and I will praise him,
my father's God, and I will exalt him.

Exodus 15:2

I will sing of your strength,
in the morning I will sing of your love;
for you are my fortress,
my refuge in times of trouble.

Psalm 59:16

The LORD is my strength and my shield;
my heart trusts in him, and I am helped.

Psalm 28:7

It is God who arms me with strength
and makes my way perfect.
He makes my feet like the feet of a deer;
he enables me to stand on the heights.

2 *Samuel* 22:33-34

Blessed are those whose strength is in you,
who have set their hearts on pilgrimage.
As they pass through the Valley of Baca,
they make it a place of springs;
the autumn rains also cover it with pools.
They go from strength to strength,
till each appears before God in Zion.

Psalm 84:5-7

You will keep in perfect peace
him whose mind is steadfast,
because he trust in you.
Trust in the LORD forever,
for the LORD, the LORD, is the Rock eternal.

Isaiah 26:3-4

Jesus said, "Come to me, all you who are weary and burdened, and I will give you rest. Take my yoke upon you and learn from me, for I am gentle and humble in heart, and you will find rest for your souls. For my yoke is easy and my burden is light."

Matthew 11:28-30

This is what the Sovereign LORD, the Holy One of Israel, says: "In repentance and rest is your salvation, in quietness and trust is your strength."

Isaiah 30:15

By the seventh day God had finished the work he had been doing; so on the seventh day he rested from all his work.

Genesis 2:2

Cast your cares on the LORD
and he will sustain you;
he will never let the righteous fall.

Psalm 55:22

Submit to God and be at peace with him;
in this way prosperity will come to you.

Job 22:21

May the Lord of peace himself give you peace at all times and in every way. The Lord be with all of you.

2 *Thessalonians* 3:16

The LORD will be your confidence
and will keep your foot from being snared.

Proverbs 3:26

Honor the LORD with your wealth;
with the firstfruits of all your crops;
then your barns will be filled to overflowing,
and your vats will brim over with new wine.

Proverbs 3:9-10

The Lord answered, "Who then is the faithful and wise manager, whom the master puts in charge of his servants to give them their food allowance at the proper time? It will be good for that servant whom the master finds doing so when he returns."

Luke 12:42-43

Good will come to him who is generous and
lends freely,
who conducts his affairs with justice.

Psalm 112:5

It is required that those who have been given a trust must prove faithful.

1 Corinthians 4:2

"Bring the whole tithe into the storehouse, that there may be food in my house. Test me in this," says the LORD Almighty, "and see if I will not throw open the floodgates of heaven and pour out so much blessing that you will not have room enough for it."

Malachi 3:10

Each one should use whatever gift he has received to serve others, faithfully administering God's grace in its various forms. If anyone speaks, he should do it as one speaking the very words of God. If anyone serves, he should do it with the strength God provides, so that in all things God may be praised through Jesus Christ.

1 *Peter* 4:10-11

May God give you the desire of your heart
and make all your plans succeed.
We will shout for joy when you are victorious
and will lift up our banners in the name of
our God.
May the LORD grant all your requests.

Psalm 20:4-5

Humility and the fear of the LORD
bring wealth and honor and life.

Proverbs 22:4

Commit to the LORD whatever you do,
and your plans will succeed.

Proverbs 16:3

Plans fail for lack of counsel,
but with many advisers they succeed.

Proverbs 15:22

Do not let this Book of the Law depart from your mouth; meditate on it day and night, so that you may be careful to do everything written in it. Then you will be prosperous and successful. Have I not commanded you? Be strong and courageous. Do not be terrified; do not be discouraged, for the LORD your God will be with you wherever you go.

Joshua 1:8-9

Blessed is the man who fears the LORD,
who finds great delight in his commands.
His children will be mighty in the land;
the generation of the upright will be blessed.
Wealth and riches are in his house,
and his righteousness endures forever.

Psalm 112:1-3

We have different gifts, according to the grace given us. If a man's gift is prophesying, let him use it in proportion to his faith. If it is serving, let him serve; if it is teaching, let him teach; if it is encouraging, let him encourage; if it is contributing to the needs of others, let him give generously; if it is leadership, let him govern diligently; if it is showing mercy, let him do it cheerfully.

Romans 12:6-8

Every good and perfect gift is from above, coming down from the Father of the heavenly lights, who does not change like shifting shadows.

James 1:17

God's gifts and his call are irrevocable.

Romans 11:29

Each man has his own gift from God; one has this gift, another has that.

1 Corinthians 7:7

There are different kinds of gifts, but the same Spirit. There are different kinds of service, but the same Lord. There are different kinds of working, but the same God works all of them in all men. Now to each one the manifestation of the Spirit is given for the common good.

1 Corinthians 12:4-7

Each one should use whatever gift he has received to serve others, faithfully administering God's grace in its various forms. If anyone speaks, he should do it as one speaking the very words of God. If anyone serves, he should do it with the strength God provides.

1 Peter 4:10-11

No temptation has seized you except what is common to man. And God is faithful; he will not let you be tempted beyond that you can bear. But when you are tempted, he will also provide a way out so that you can stand up under it.

1 Corinthians 10:13

Submit yourselves, then, to God. Resist the devil, and he will flee from you

James 4:7

Because Jesus himself suffered when he was tempted, he is able to help those who are being tempted.

Hebrews 2:18

Be strong in the Lord and in his mighty power. Put on the full armor of God so that you can take your stand against the devil's schemes.

Ephesians 6:10-11

It is for freedom that Christ has set us free. Stand firm, then, and do not let yourselves be burdened again by a yoke of slavery.

Galatians 5:1

Since we have a great high priest who has gone through the heavens, Jesus the Son of God, let us hold firmly to the faith we profess. For we do not have a high priest who is unable to sympathize with our weaknesses, but we have one who has been tempted in every way, just as we are—yet was without sin. Let us then approach the throne of grace with confidence, so that we may receive mercy and find grace to help in our time of need.

Hebrews 4:14-16

Thanks be to God for his indescribable gift!

2 Corinthians 9:15

In everything, by prayer and petition, with thanksgiving, present your requests to God. And the peace of God, which transcends all understanding, will guard your hearts and your minds in Christ Jesus.

Philippians 4:6-7

Since we are receiving a kingdom that cannot be shaken, let us be thankful, and so worship God acceptably with reverence and awe.

Hebrews 12:28

Just as you received Christ Jesus as Lord, continue to live in him, rooted and built up in him, strengthened in the faith as you were taught, and overflowing with thankfulness.

Colossians 2:6-7

Thanks be to God! He gives us the victory through our Lord Jesus Christ.

1 Corinthians 15:57

Give thanks in all circumstances, for this is God's will for you in Christ Jesus.

1 Thessalonians 5:18

Let the word of Christ dwell in you richly as you teach and admonish one another with all wisdom, and as you sing psalms, hymns and spiritual songs with gratitude in your hearts to God.

Colossians 3:16

Let them give thanks to the LORD for his
        unfailing love
    and his wonderful deeds for men,
for he satisfies the thirsty
    and fills the hungry with good things.

Psalm 107:8-9

The LORD is my strength and my shield;
    my heart trusts in him, and I am helped.
My heart leaps for joy
    and I will give thanks to him in song.

Psalm 28:7

The mind of sinful man is death, but he mind controlled by the Spirit is life and peace.

Romans 8:6

The wisdom of the prudent is to give thought to their ways.

Proverbs 14:8

Whatever is true, whatever is noble, whatever is right, whatever is pure, whatever is lovely, whatever is admirable—if anything is excellent or praiseworthy—think about such things.

Philippians 4:8

How precious to me are your thoughts, O God!
    How vast is the sum of them!
Were I to count them,
    they would outnumber the grains of sand.

Psalm 139:17–18

Be clear minded and self-controlled so that you can pray.

1 Peter 4:7

"I the LORD search the heart
and examine the mind,
to reward a man according to his conduct,
according to what his deeds deserve."

Jeremiah 17:10

We demolish arguments and every pretension that sets itself up against the knowledge of God, and we take captive every thought to make it obedient to Christ.

2 *Corinthians* 10:5

The LORD knows the thoughts of man.

Psalm 94:11

Holy brothers, who share in the heavenly calling, fix your thoughts on Jesus, the apostle and high priest whom we confess.

Hebrews 3:1

"My thoughts are not your thoughts,
neither are your ways my ways,"
declares the LORD.

Isaiah 55:8

Blessed is the man who perseveres under trial, because when he has stood the test, he will receive the crown of life that God has promised to those who love him.

James 1:12

Do not be surprised at the painful trial you are suffering, as though something strange were happening to you. But rejoice that you participate in the sufferings of Christ, so that you may be overjoyed when his glory is revealed. If you are insulted because of the name of Christ, you are blessed, for the Spirit of glory and of God rests on you

1 Peter 4:12-14

We are not trying to please men but God, who tests our hearts.

1 Thessalonians 2:4

Consider it all joy, my brothers, whenever you face trials of many kinds, because you know that the testing of your faith develops perseverance.

James 1:2-3

The God of all grace, who called you to his eternal glory in Christ, after you have suffered a little while, will himself restore you and make you strong, firm and steadfast.

1 Peter 5:10

I consider that our present sufferings are not worth comparing with the glory that will be revealed in us.

Romans 8:18

Test me, O LORD, and try me,
examine my heart and my mind;
for your love is ever before me,
and I walk continually in your truth.

Psalm 26:2-3

You are my hiding place, LORD;
you will protect me from trouble
and surround me with songs of deliverance.

Psalm 32:7

Our light and momentary troubles are achieving for us an eternal glory that far outweighs them all.

2 Corinthians 4:17

Praise be to the God and Father of our Lord Jesus Christ, the Father of compassion and the God of all comfort, who comforts us in all our troubles, so that we can comfort those in any trouble with the comfort we ourselves have received from God.

2 Corinthians 1:3-4

A righteous man may have many troubles,
but the LORD delivers him from them all.

Psalm 34:19

"Because he loves me," says the LORD,
"I will rescue him;
I will protect him, for he acknowledges
my name.
He will call upon me, and I will answer him;
I will be with him in trouble,
I will deliver him and honor him."

Psalm 91:14-15

Though I walk in the midst of trouble,
you preserve my life, LORD;
you stretch out your hand against the anger of
my foes
with your right hand you save me.

Psalm 138:7

Jesus said, "Do not let your hearts be troubled.
Trust in God; trust also in me."

John 14:1

Jesus said, "In this world you will have trouble.
But take heart! I have overcome the world."

John 16:33

Blessed is the man who trusts in the LORD,
whose confidence is in him.
He will be like a tree planted by the water
that sends out its roots by the stream.
It does not fear when heat comes;
its leaves are always green.
It has no worries in a year of drought
and never fails to bear fruit.

Jeremiah 17:7-8

Trust in the LORD with all your heart
and lean not on your own understanding;
in all your ways acknowledge him,
and he will make your paths straight.

Proverbs 3:5-6

Trust in the LORD and do good;
dwell in the land and enjoy safe pasture.

Psalm 37:3

He who trusts in the LORD will prosper.

Proverbs 28:25

Those who trust in the LORD are like
Mount Zion,
which cannot be shaken but endures forever.
As the mountains surround Jerusalem,
so the LORD surrounds his people
both now and forevermore.

Psalm 125:1-2

You will keep in perfect peace
him whose mind is steadfast,
because he trusts in you.
Trust in the LORD forever,
for the LORD, the LORD, is the Rock eternal.

Isaiah 26:3-4

Blessed is the man
who makes the LORD his trust,
who does not look to the proud,
to those who turn aside to false gods.

Psalm 40:4

Anyone who trusts in Christ will never be put to shame.

Romans 10:11

Many are the woes of the wicked,
but the LORD's unfailing love
surrounds the man who trusts in him.

Psalm 32:10

Fear of man will prove to be a snare,
but whoever trusts in the LORD is kept safe.

Proverbs 29:25

Whoever gives heed to instruction prospers,
and blessed is he who trusts in the LORD.

Proverbs 16:20

Those who know your name will trust in you,
for you, LORD, have never forsaken those
who seek you.

Psalm 9:10

It is better to take refuge in the LORD
than to trust in man.
It is better to take refuge in the LORD
than to trust in princes.

Psalm 118:8-9

May the God of hope fill you with all joy and peace as you trust in him, so that you may overflow with hope by the power of the Holy Spirit.

Romans 15:13

Some trust in chariots and some in horses,
but we trust in the name of the LORD
our God.
They are brought to their knees and fall,
but we rise up and stand firm.

Psalm 20:7-8

He who dwells in the shelter of the Most High
will rest in the shadow of the Almighty.
I will say of the LORD, "He is my refuge and my
fortress
my God, in whom I trust."

Psalm 91:1-2

To the Jews who had believed him, Jesus said, "If you hold to my teaching, you are really my disciples. Then you will know the truth, and the truth will set you free."

John 8:31-32

Buy the truth and do not sell it;
get wisdom, discipline and understanding.

Proverbs 23:23

Jesus said, "I have much more to say to you, more than you can now bear. But when he, the Spirit of truth, comes, he will guide you into all truth. He will not speak on his own; he will speak only what he hears, and he will tell you what is yet to come."

John 16:12-13

Jesus answered, "I am the way and the truth and the life. No one comes to the Father except through me."

John 14:6

We know that we are children of God, and that the whole world is under the control of the evil one. We know also that the Son of God has come and has given us understanding, so that we may know him who is true. And we are in him who is true—even in his Son Jesus Christ. He is the true God and eternal life.

1 John 5:19-20

"You are a king, then!" said Pilate.
Jesus answered, "You are right in saying I am a king. In fact, for this reason I was born, and for this I came into the world to testify to the truth. Everyone on the side of truth listens to me."

John 18:37

My purpose is that they may be encouraged in heart and united in love, so that they may have the full riches of complete understanding, in order that they may know the mystery of God, namely, Christ, in whom are hidden all the treasures of wisdom and knowledge.

Colossians 2:2-3

I have more understanding than the elders,
for I obey your precepts. ...
I gain understanding from your precepts.

Psalm 119:100, 104

Though it cost all you have, get understanding.
Esteem her, and she will exalt you;
embrace her, and she will honor you.
She will set a garland of grace on your head
and present you with a crown of splendor.

Proverbs 4:7-9

Blessed is the man who finds wisdom,
the man who gains understanding,
for she is more profitable than silver
and yields better returns than gold.
She is more precious than rubies;
nothing you desire can compare with her.
Long life is in her right hand;
in her left hand are riches and honor.
Her ways are pleasant ways,
and all her paths are peace.
She is a tree of life to those who embrace her;
those who lay hold of her will be blessed.

Proverbs 3:13-18

Who is wise and understanding among you? Let him show it by his good life, by deeds done in the humility that comes from wisdom.

James 3:13

He who cherishes understanding prospers.

Proverbs 19:8

It was God who gave some to be apostles, some to be prophets, some to be evangelists, and some to be pastors and teachers, to prepare God's people for works of service, so that the body of Christ may be built up until we all reach unity in the faith and in the knowledge of the Son of God and become mature, attaining to the whole measure of the fullness of Christ.

Ephesians 4:11-13

Jesus said, "I pray also for those who will believe in me through [my disciples'] message. May they be brought to complete unity to let the world know that you sent me."

John 17:20-21

Agree with one another so that there may be no divisions among you and that you may be perfectly united in mind and thought.

1 Corinthians 1:10

Make every effort to keep the unity of the Spirit.

Ephesians 4:3

How good and pleasant it is
when brothers live together in unity!
It is like precious oil poured on the head,
running down on the beard,
running down on Aaron's beard,
down upon the collar of his robes.
It is as if the dew of Hermon
were falling on Mount Zion.
For there the LORD bestows his blessing,
even life forevermore.

Psalm 133

Live in harmony with one another; be sympathetic, love as brothers, be compassionate and humble. Do not repay evil with evil or insult with insult, but with blessing, because to this you were called so that you may inherit a blessing.

1 Peter 3:8-9

Turn my heart toward your statutes, LORD,
and not toward selfish gain.
Turn my eyes away from worthless things;
preserve my life according to your word.

Psalm 119:36-37

Do nothing out of selfish ambition or vain conceit, but in humility consider others better than yourselves. Each of you should look not only to your own interests, but also to the interest of others.

Philippians 2:3-4

Love is patient, love is kind. It does not envy, it does not boast, it is not proud. It is not rude, it is not self-seeking, it is not easily angered, it keeps no record of wrongs.

1 Corinthians 13:4-5

If you harbor bitter envy and selfish ambition in your hearts, do not boast about it or deny the truth. Such "wisdom" does not come down from heaven, but is earthly, unspiritual, of the devil. For where you have envy and selfish ambition, there you find disorder and every evil practice. But the wisdom that comes from heaven is first of all pure; then peace-loving, considerate, submissive, full of mercy and good fruit, impartial and sincere. Peacemakers who sow in peace raise a harvest of righteousness.

James 3:14-18

Jesus said, "Watch out! Be on your guard against all kinds of greed; a man's life does not consist in the abundance of his possessions."

Luke 12:15

Whatever is true, whatever is noble, whatever is right, whatever is pure, whatever is lovely, whatever is admirable—if anything is excellent or praiseworthy—think about such things.

Philippians 4:8

Be careful that you do not forget the LORD your God, failing to observe his commands, his laws and his decrees. ... Otherwise, when you eat and are satisfied, when you build fine houses and settle down, and when your herds and flocks grow large and your silver and gold increase and all you have is multiplied, then your heart will become proud and you will forget the LORD your God.

Deuteronomy 8:11-14

Jesus said, "Do to others as you would have them do to you."

Luke 6:31

By faith Moses, when he had grown up, refused to be known as the Son of Pharaoh's daughter. He chose to be mistreated along with the people of God rather than to enjoy the pleasures of sin for a short time. He regarded disgrace for the sake of Christ as of greater value than the treasures of Egypt, because he was looking ahead to his reward.

Hebrews 11:24-26

Who may ascend the hill of the LORD?
Who may stand in his holy place?
He who has clean hands and a pure heart,
who does not lift up his soul to an idol
or swear by what is false.
He will receive blessing from the LORD
and vindication from God his Savior.

Psalm 24:3-5

God's commands are not burdensome, for everyone born of God overcomes the world. This is the victory that has overcome the world, even our faith. Who is it that overcomes the world? Only he who believes that Jesus is the Son of God.

1 John 5:3-5

We will not all sleep, but we will all be changed—in a flash, in the twinkling of an eye, at the last trumpet. For the trumpet will sound, the dead will be raised imperishable, and we will be changed. ... Then the saying that is written will come true: "Death has been swallowed up in victory." ... Thanks be to God! He gives us the victory through our Lord Jesus Christ.

1 Corinthians 15:51, 54, 57

God holds victory in store for the upright,
he is a shield to those whose walk is blameless,
for he guards the course of the just
and protects the way of his faithful ones.

Proverbs 2:7-8

There is no wisdom, no insight, no plan
that can succeed against the LORD.
The horse is made ready for the day of battle,
but victory rests with the LORD.

Proverbs 21:30-31

With God we will gain the victory,
and he will trample down our enemies.

Psalm 60:12

Who shall separate us from the love of Christ? Shall trouble or hardship or persecution or famine or nakedness or danger or sword? ... No, in all these things we are more than conquerors through him who loved us.

Romans 8:35, 37

Jesus said, "In this world you will have trouble. But take heart! I have overcome the world."

John 16:33

The blessing of the LORD brings wealth,
and he adds no trouble to it.

Proverbs 10:22

Command those who are rich in this present world not to be arrogant nor to put their hope in wealth, which is so uncertain, but to put their hope in God, who richly provides us with everything for our enjoyment. Command them to do good, to be rich in good deeds, and to be generous and willing to share. In this way they will lay up treasure for themselves as a firm foundation for the coming age, so that they may take hold of the life that is truly life.

1 *Timothy* 6:17-19

Honor the LORD with your wealth,
with the firstfruits of all your crops;
then your barns will be filled to overflowing,
and your vats will brim over with new wine.

Proverbs 3:9–10

Remember the LORD your God, for it is he who gives you the ability to produce wealth, and so confirms his covenant, which he swore to your forefathers, as it is today.

Deuteronomy 8:18

Rich and poor have this in common:
The LORD is the maker of them all.

Proverbs 22:2

Has not God chosen those who are poor in the eyes of the world to be rich in faith and to inherit the kingdom he promised those who love him?

James 2:5

Do not forsake wisdom, and she will protect
you;
love her, and she will watch over you.
Wisdom is supreme; therefore get wisdom.

Proverbs 4:6-7

If any of you lacks wisdom, he should ask God, who gives generously to all without finding fault, and it will be given to him.

James 1:5

I guide you in the way of wisdom
and lead you along straight paths.
When you walk, your steps will not be
hampered;
when you run, you will not stumble.

Proverbs 4:11-12

The wisdom that comes from heaven is first of all pure; then peace-loving, considerate, submissive, full of mercy and good fruit, impartial and sincere.

James 3:17

The foolishness of God is wiser than man's wisdom, and the weakness of God is stronger than man's strength.

1 Corinthians 1:25

Wisdom, like an inheritance, is a good thing
and benefits those who see the sun.
Wisdom is a shelter
as money is a shelter,
but the advantage of knowledge is this:
that wisdom preserves the life of its possessor.

Ecclesiastes 7:11-12

The fear of the LORD is the beginning of wisdom;
all who follow his precepts have good understanding.
To him belongs eternal praise.

Psalm 111:10

Wisdom is sweet to your soul;
if you find it, there is a future hope for you,
and your hope will not be cut off.

Proverbs 24:14

All hard work brings a profit.

Proverbs 14:23

God is not unjust; he will not forget your work and the love you have shown him as you have helped his people and continue to help them.

Hebrews 6:10

Stand firm. Let nothing move you. Always give yourselves fully to the work of the Lord, because you know that your labor in the Lord is not in vain.

1 Corinthians 15:58

Jesus said, "Do not work for food that spoils, but for food that endures to eternal life, which the Son of Man will give you. On him God the Father has placed his seal of approval."

John 6:27

Whatever you do, work at it with all your heart, as working for the Lord, not for men, since you know that you will receive an inheritance from the Lord as a reward.

Colossians 3:23-24

Don't you know that those who work in the temple get their food from the temple, and those who serve at the altar share in what is offered on the altar? In the same way, the Lord has commanded that those who preach the gospel should receive their living from the gospel.

1 Corinthians 9:13-14

The sluggard craves and gets nothing,
but the desires of the diligent are fully
satisfied.

Proverbs 13:4

Lazy hands make a man poor,
but diligent hands bring wealth.

Proverbs 10:4

Since we are surrounded by such a great cloud of witnesses, let us throw off everything that hinders and the sin that so easily entangles, and let us run with perseverance the race marked out for us. Let us fix our eyes on Jesus, the author and perfecter of our faith, who for the joy set before him endured the cross, scorning its shame, and sat down at the right hand of the throne of God. Consider him who endured such opposition from sinful men, so that you will not grow weary and lose heart.

Hebrews 12:1–3

The hour has come for you to wake up from your slumber, because our salvation is nearer now than when we first believed. The night is nearly over; the day is almost here. So let us put aside the deeds of darkness and put on the armor of light.

Romans 13:11–12

God was reconciling the world to himself in Christ, not counting men's sins against them. And he has committed to us the message of reconciliation. We are therefore Christ's ambassadors, as though God were making his appeal through us.

2 Corinthians 5:19-20

Be confident of this, that he who began a good work in you will carry it on to completion until the day of Christ Jesus.

Philippians 1:6

Remember the LORD your God, for it is he who gives you the ability to produce wealth, and so confirms his covenant, which he swore to your forefathers, as it is today.

Deuteronomy 8:18

Jesus said, "Do not work for food that spoils, but for food that endures to eternal life, which the Son of Man will give you. On him God the Father has placed his seal of approval."

John 6:27

Whatever you do, work at it with all your heart, as working for the Lord, not for men, since you know that you will receive an inheritance from the Lord as a reward.

Colossians 3:23-24

"I know the plans I have for you," declares the LORD, "plans to prosper you and not to harm you, plans to give you hope and a future."

Jeremiah 29:11

May God give you the desire of your heart
and make all your plans succeed.
We will shout for joy when you are victorious
and will lift up our banners in the name of
our God.
May the LORD grant all your requests.

Psalm 20:4-5

May the God of hope fill you with all joy and peace as you trust in him, so that you may overflow with hope by the power of the Holy Spirit.

Romans 15:13

We want to hear from you. Please send your comments about this book to us in care of zreview@zondervan.com. Thank you.

ZONDERVAN.com/
AUTHORTRACKER
follow your favorite authors